AF618520

NATHLIE PROVÔSTY

This catalogue is published on the occasion of the exhibition *(the third ear)*
March 30 – May 15, 2016
Nathalie Karg Gallery
291 Grand Street, New York, NY 10002

Cover design by Faconti & Richer

Design by Elissa Medina and Faconti & Richer

Image editing by David La Spina, Esto Photographics

Text by Jarrett Earnest

Production management by Sonja Bahr

Production by DZA Druckerei zu Altenburg GmbH

All images credited to Christopher Gardner, except pp. 2, 3, 75, 81, 83, 85 to Zack Garlitos

Cover: *Twice Six*, 2016 (detail)

Special thanks to Nathalie Karg, Clifford Ross, Phong Bui, Jarrett Earnest, Elissa Medina, Claudia Arzeno, Rob de Oude, Erica Fenaroli, Chiara Rusconi, Francesca Migliorati, Dana Faconti, Francesca Richer, David La Spina, Larissa Bischoff, Uta Grosenick, Dan Crews, Christopher Gardner, Michael Straus, and Alex McClave

Distribution by Gestalten, Berlin
www.gestalten.com
sales@gestalten.com

ISBN 978-3-95476-165-4
Printed in Germany

Published by DISTANZ Verlag
www.distanz.de

NATHLIE PROVOSTY

Born 1981 in Cincinnati, Ohio
Lives and works in Brooklyn, New York

SOLO EXHIBITIONS

2016 *(the third ear)*, Nathalie Karg Gallery, New York, NY
2015 Jablonka Maruani Mercier Gallery Project Space, Knokke, Belgium
2013 *Violets Violence Silence*, Diet, Miami, FL
2012 *Book of Hours*, 1:1, New York, NY
2011 *Green(ish) Hermeticism*, Diet, Miami, FL

SELECTED GROUP EXHIBITIONS

2016 *A Way of Living*, A Palazzo Gallery, Brescia, Italy

2015 *Neon Eon*, Kate Werble Gallery, New York, NY
Is This This That, Part II, Greene Exhibitions, Los Angeles, CA
Ultraviolet, Diet, Miami, FL
Painting the Sky Blue, Stefan Lundgren Gallery, Mallorca, Spain
RE(a)D, Nathalie Karg Gallery, New York, NY
Abstract Index, Galerie Ruth Leuchter, Dusseldorf, Germany
Politics of Surface, Berthold Pott, Cologne, Germany
Soft Opening, Mihai Nicodim, Los Angeles, CA

2014 *173 East 94th Street / Chaussée de Waterloo 550*, Middlemarch, Brussels, Belgium
Rituals, Larm Galleri, Copenhagen, Denmark
Nathlie Provosty & Ann Pibal, Halsey Mckay, East Hampton, NY
Simplest Means, Jeff Bailey, New York, NY
Night Tide, Diet, Miami, FL
All the Best Artists Are My Friends, curated by Ray Smith, Mana Contemporary, Jersey City, NJ

2013 *Correspondences: Ad Reinhardt at 100*, Temp Gallery, New York, NY
Mia Goyette, Siobhan Liddell, Jo Nigoghossian, Nathlie Provosty, Greene Exhibitions, Los Angeles, CA
Paint On, Paint Off, Halsey Mckay Gallery, East Hampton, NY
Banter, Diet, curated by James Cope, Miami, FL
Come Together: Surviving Sandy, Dedalus Foundation, Brooklyn, NY
Atlas Points, Emery Theater Gallery, curated by Bryce Dessner, Cincinnati, OH

2012 *Prophetic Diagrams*, George and Jorgen, London, UK
Inside Out 2012, Inside Out Museum, Beijing, China
The Annual, American Academy of Arts and Letters, New York, NY
Brucennial, 159 Bleecker Street, New York, NY

2011 *Geometric Days*, Exit Art, New York, NY
What Tornado?, Microscope Gallery, Brooklyn, NY

PROLOGUE

Loop, 2015, oil on linen, diptych, 84 x 93 ½ inches (213.4 x 237.5 cm). Private Collection, Switzerland

Doubleu, 2013–2014, oil on linen, diptych, 84 x 93 ⅜ inches (213.4 x 237.2 cm). Private Collection, Los Angeles

Doubleu (pale), 2014, oil on linen, diptych, 84 x 93 ⅜ inches (213.4 x 237.2 cm). Private Collection, Palma de Majorca

Straw Man, 2014, oil on linen, 84 x 92 inches (213 x 234 cm). Private Collection, Belgium

Near Ultraviolet, 2015, oil on linen, 19 x 15 inches (48 x 38 cm). Collection of Hugh Freund, New York

Near Ultraviolet II, 2015, oil on linen, 19 x 15 inches (48 x 38 cm). Private Collection, USA

Red Herring, 2015, oil on linen, diptych, 84 x 93 ½ inches (213.4 x 237.5 cm). Private Collection, Palma de Majorca

Near Infrared III, 2015, oil on linen, 19 x 15 inches (48 x 38 cm). Rubell Family Collection, Miami

Near Infrared, 2015, oil on linen, 19 x 15 inches (48 x 38 cm). Collection of Daniel Schwartz, Miami

Near Infrared II, 2015, oil on linen, 19 x 15 inches (48 x 38 cm). Private Collection, Switzerland

Bevel VII, 2015, oil on linen, 19 x 15 inches (48 x 38 cm). Private Collection, Stockholm, Sweden

Bevel, 2014, oil on linen, 19 x 15 inches (48 x 38 cm). Private Collection, Belgium

Bevel II, 2015, oil on linen, 19 x 15 inches (48 x 38 cm). Private Collection, Belgium

Bevel IV, 2015, oil on linen, 19 x 15 inches (48 x 38 cm). Collection of David Totah, New York

Subject without a Skin, 2012–2014, oil on linen, 84 x 96 inches (213 x 244 cm). Private Collection, Belgium

Subject without a Skin II, 2014, oil on linen, 84 x 96 inches (213 x 244 cm).

Subject without a Skin III, 2014, oil on linen, 84 x 96 inches (213 x 244 cm). Private Collection, Belgium

Thrice, 2014, oil on linen, 84 x 92 inches (213 x 234 cm). Collection of Michael Straus, Birmingham

Thrice II, 2014, oil on linen, 84 x 92 inches (213 x 234 cm). Collection of Jim and Julie Taylor, Denver

Valence Violence Violets, 2013, oil on linen, diptych, 84 x 93 ⅜ inches (213.4 x 237.2 cm). Private Collection, Belgium

Violets Violence Silence, 2013, oil on linen, diptych, 84 x 93 ⅜ inches (213.4 x 237.2 cm). Thomas Family Collection, New York

(the third ear)

Council, Untitled (15-52)–(15-57), 2015, watercolor and walnut ink on paper, 8¼ x 5⅞ inches (21 x 15 cm)

Twice Six, 2016, oil on linen, 84 x 92 inches (213 x 234 cm). Collection of Clifford Ross

Gilles, 2014, oil on linen, 84 x 92 inches (213 x 234 cm). Collection of Allison Rubler, New York

West, 2016, oil on linen, 84 x 92 inches (213 x 234 cm). Private Collection

Dissonance, 2016, oil on linen, 19 x 15 inches (48 x 38 cm). Collection of Andrea Krantz and Harvey Sawikin, New York

Assonance, 2016, oil on linen, 19 x 15 inches (48 x 38 cm). Collection of Roger E. Kass, Newport

Consonance, 2016, oil on linen, 19 x 15 inches (48 x 38 cm). Private Collection, London

Consonance II, 2016, oil on linen, 19 x 15 inches (48 x 38 cm). Collection of Andrew Ginzel, New York

Resonance II, 2016, oil on linen, 19 x 15 inches (48 x 38 cm). Collection of Iris and Adam Singer, Paradise Valley

Resonance, 2016, oil on linen, 19 x 15 inches (48 x 38 cm). Collection of Marc Jancou, Switzerland

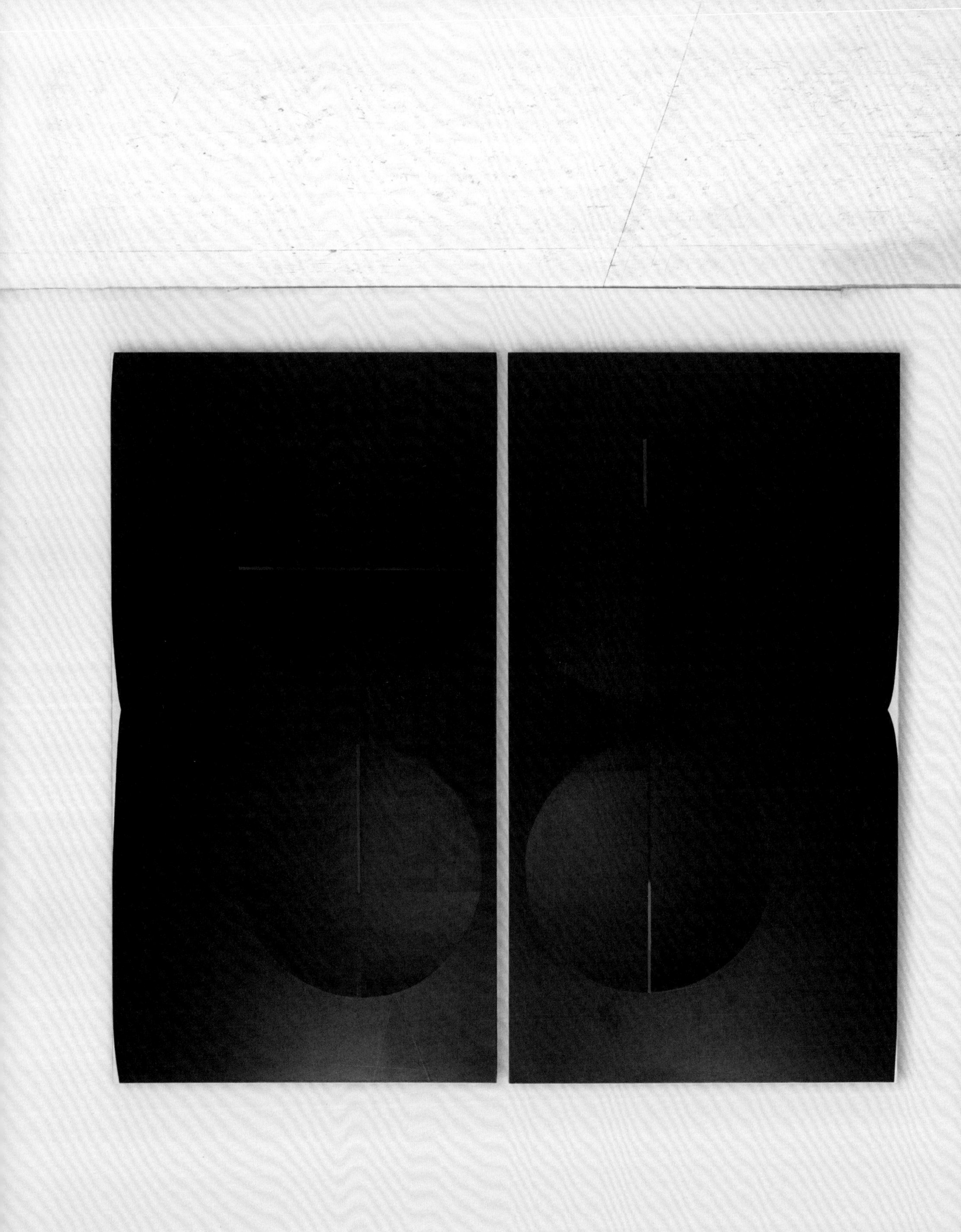

Valence Violence Violets, 2013

Violets Violence Silence, 2013

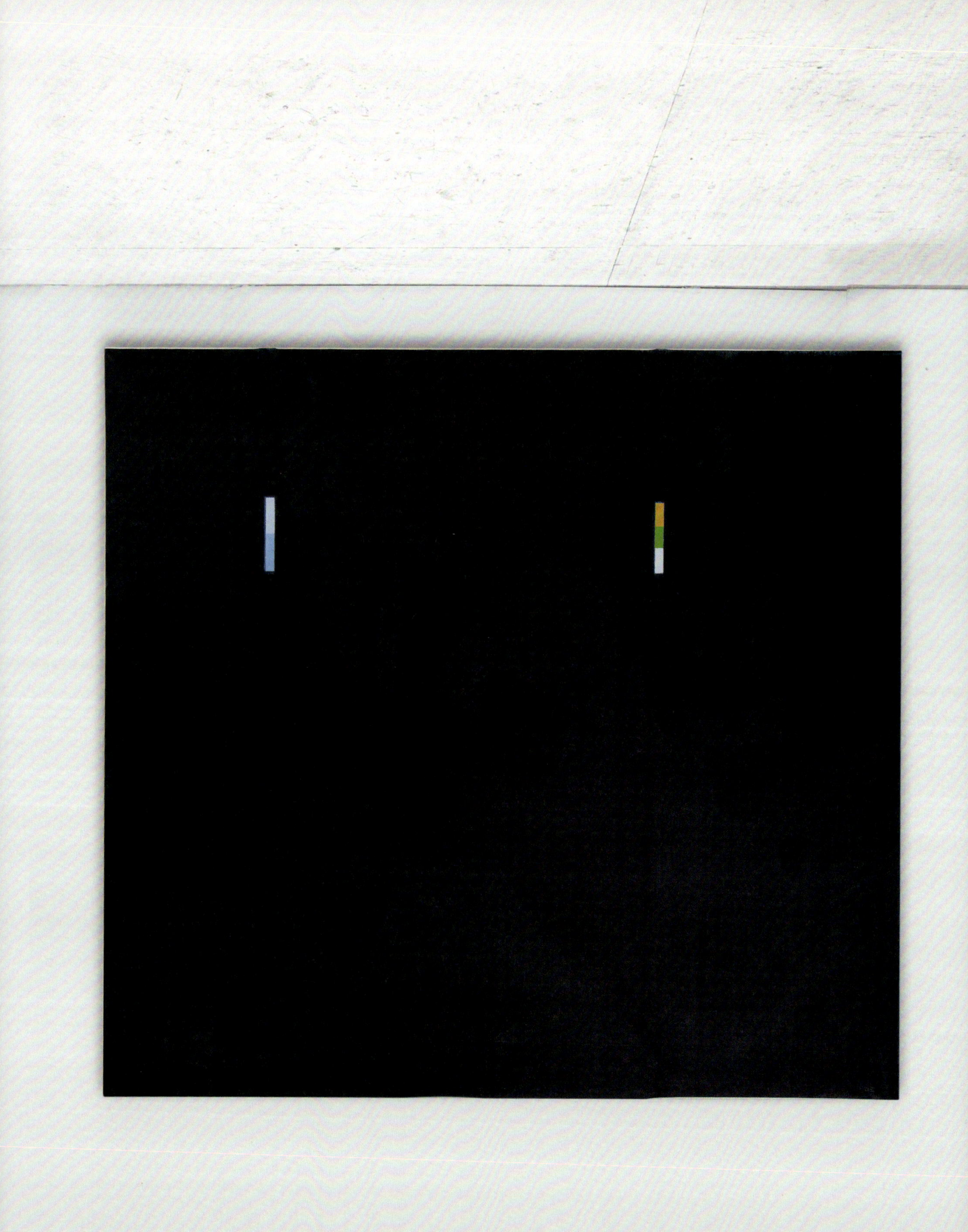

Thrice II, 2014

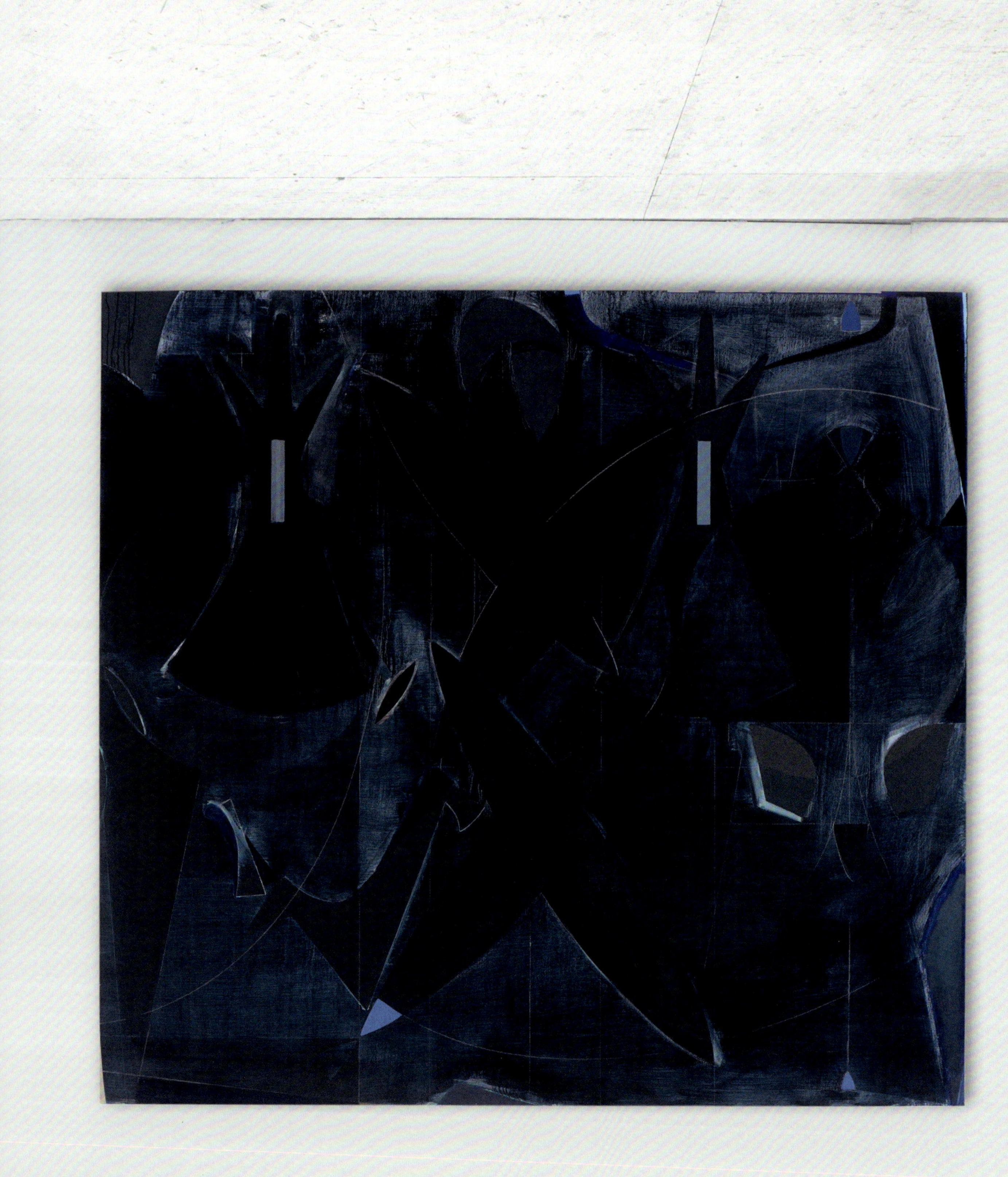

Thrice, 2014

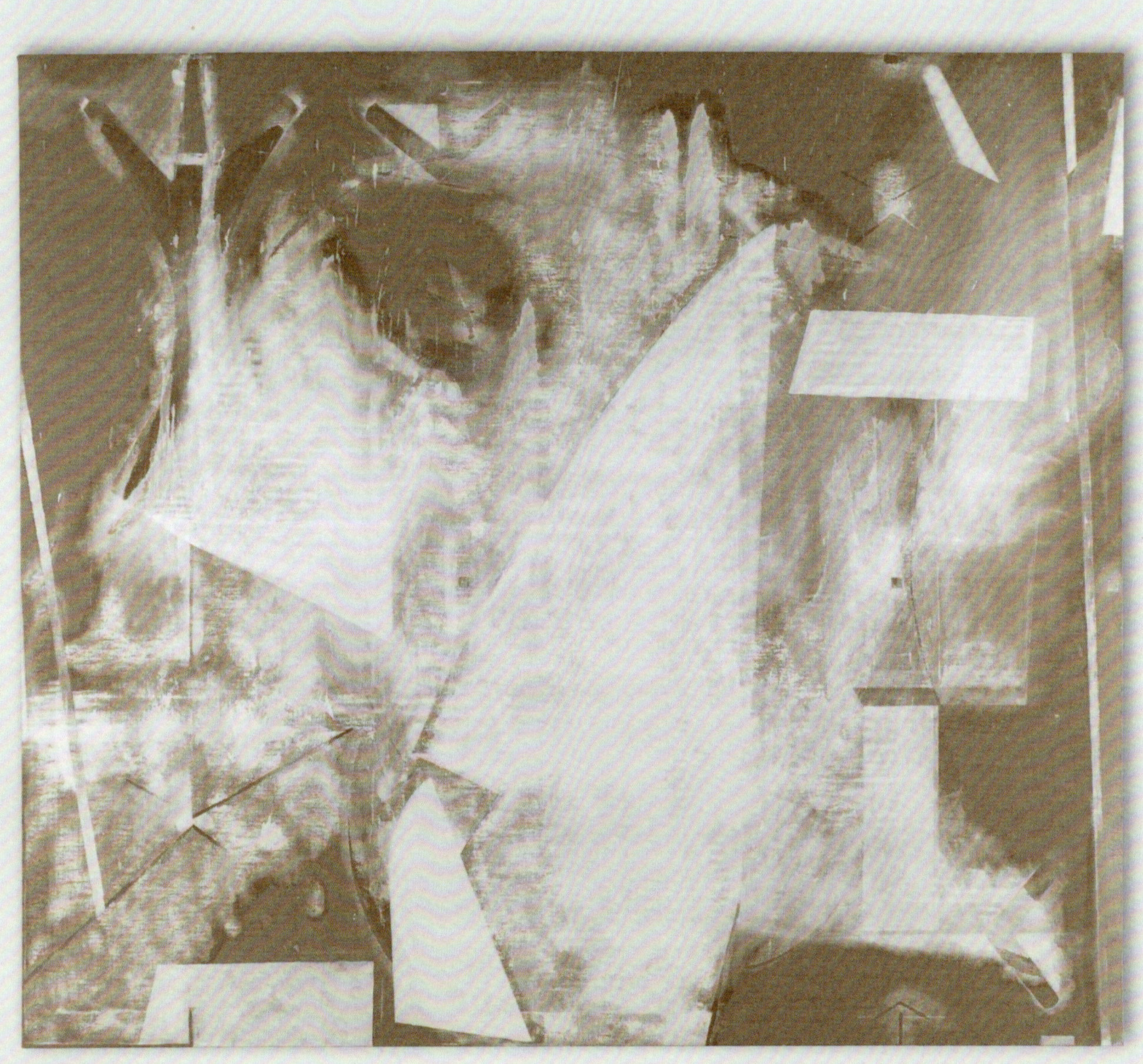

Subject Without a Skin III, 2014

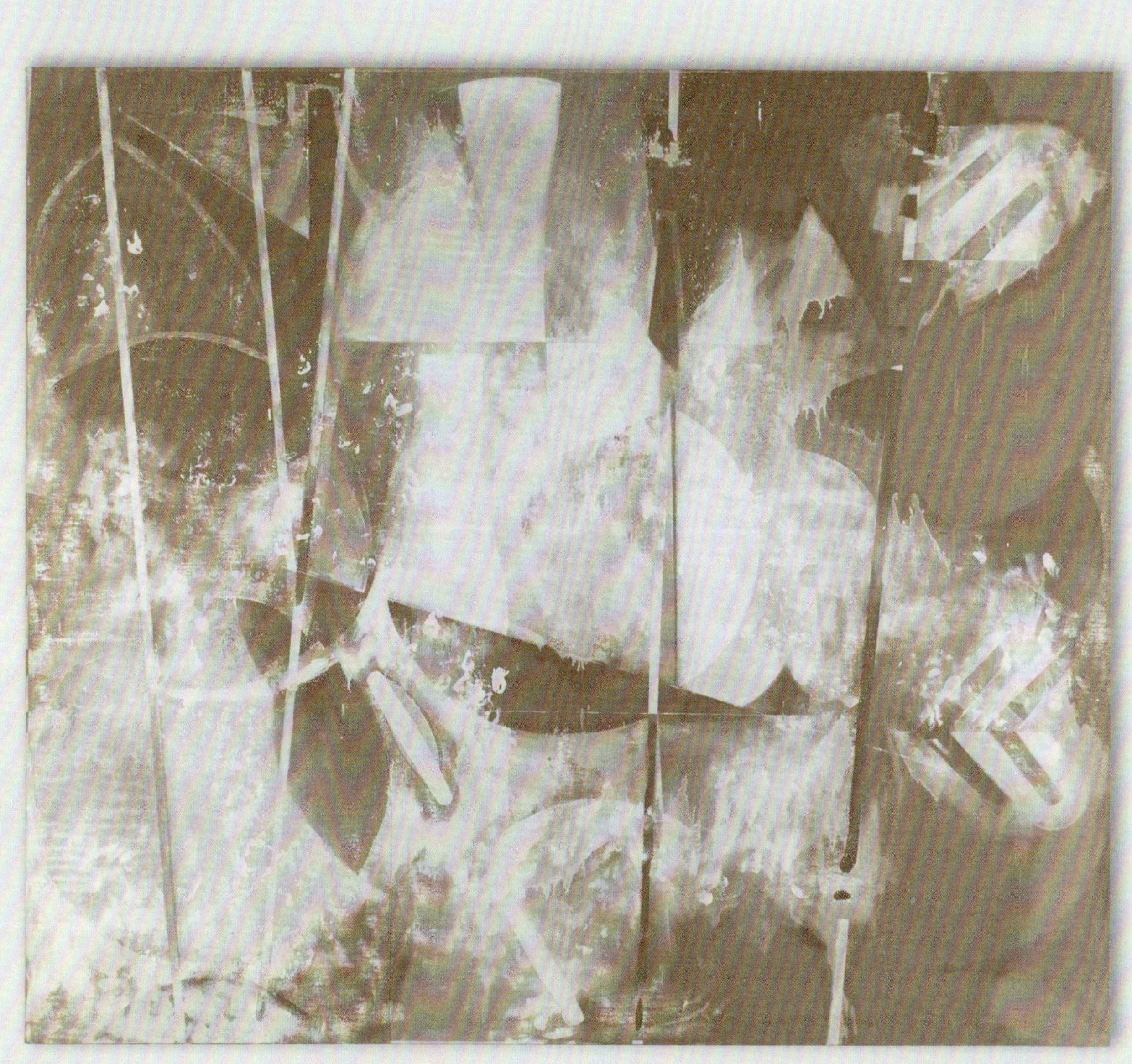

Subject Without a Skin II, 2014

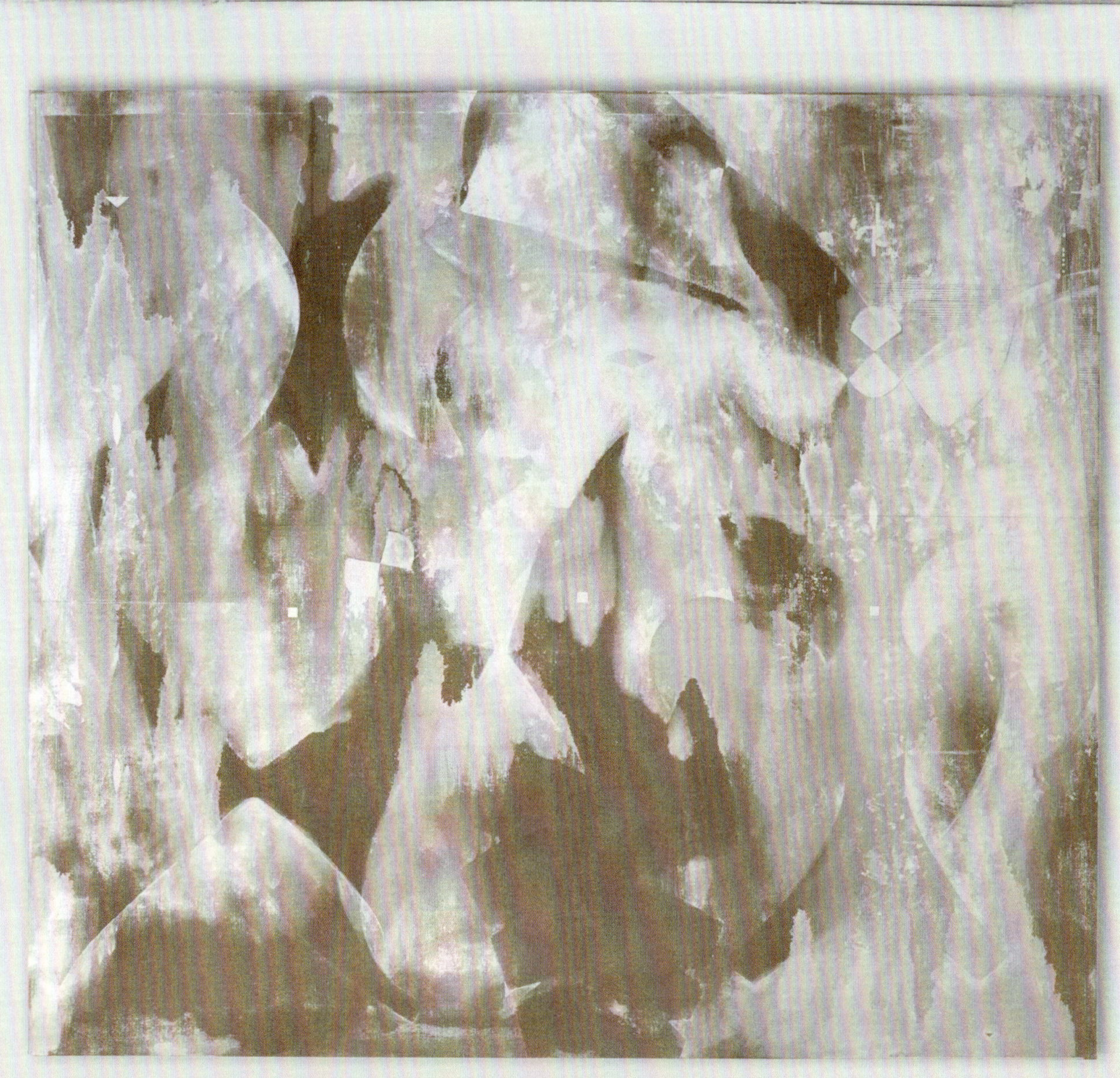

Subject Without a Skin, 2012–2014

Bevel IV, 2015

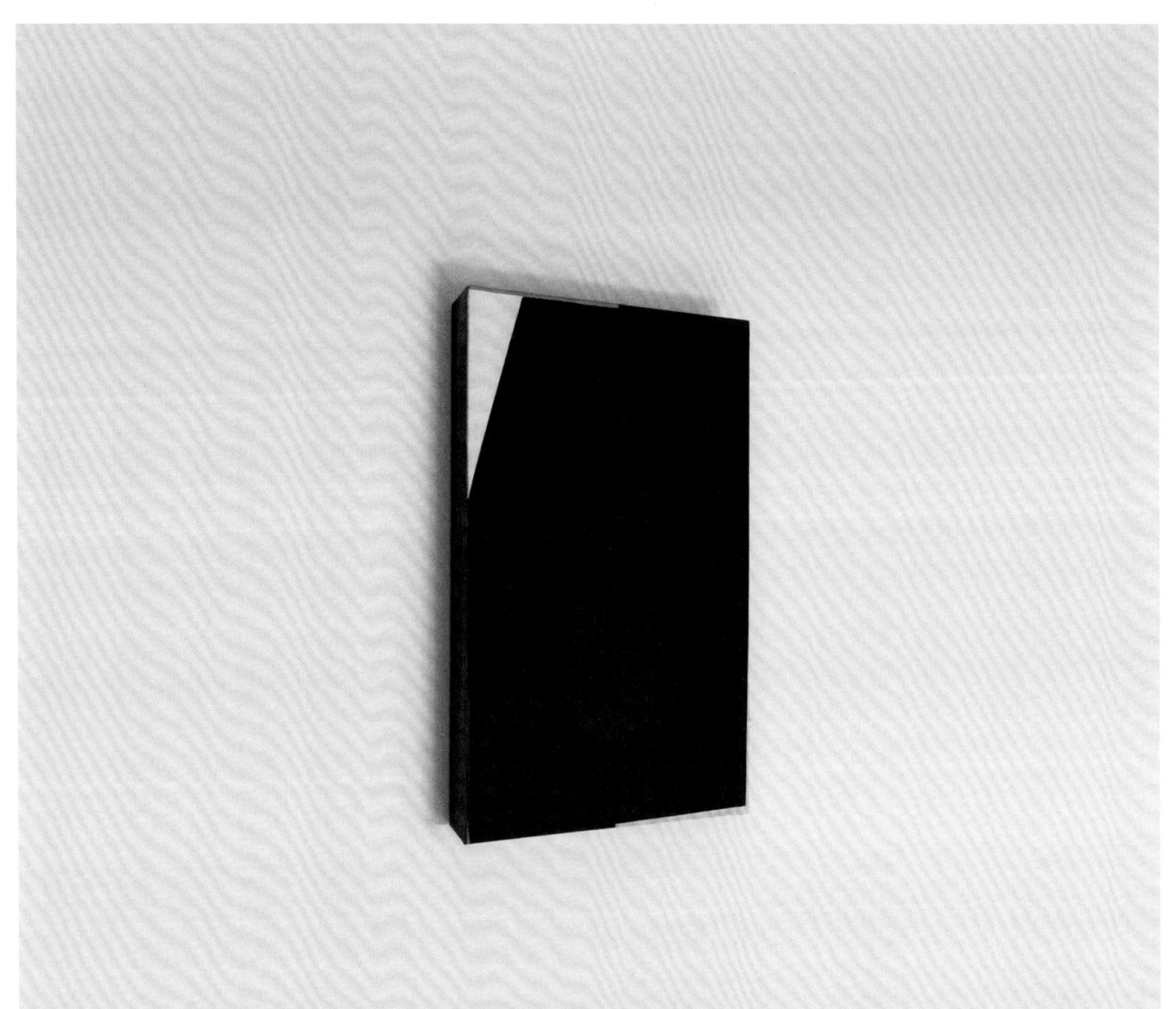

Bevel II, 2015

Bevel, 2014

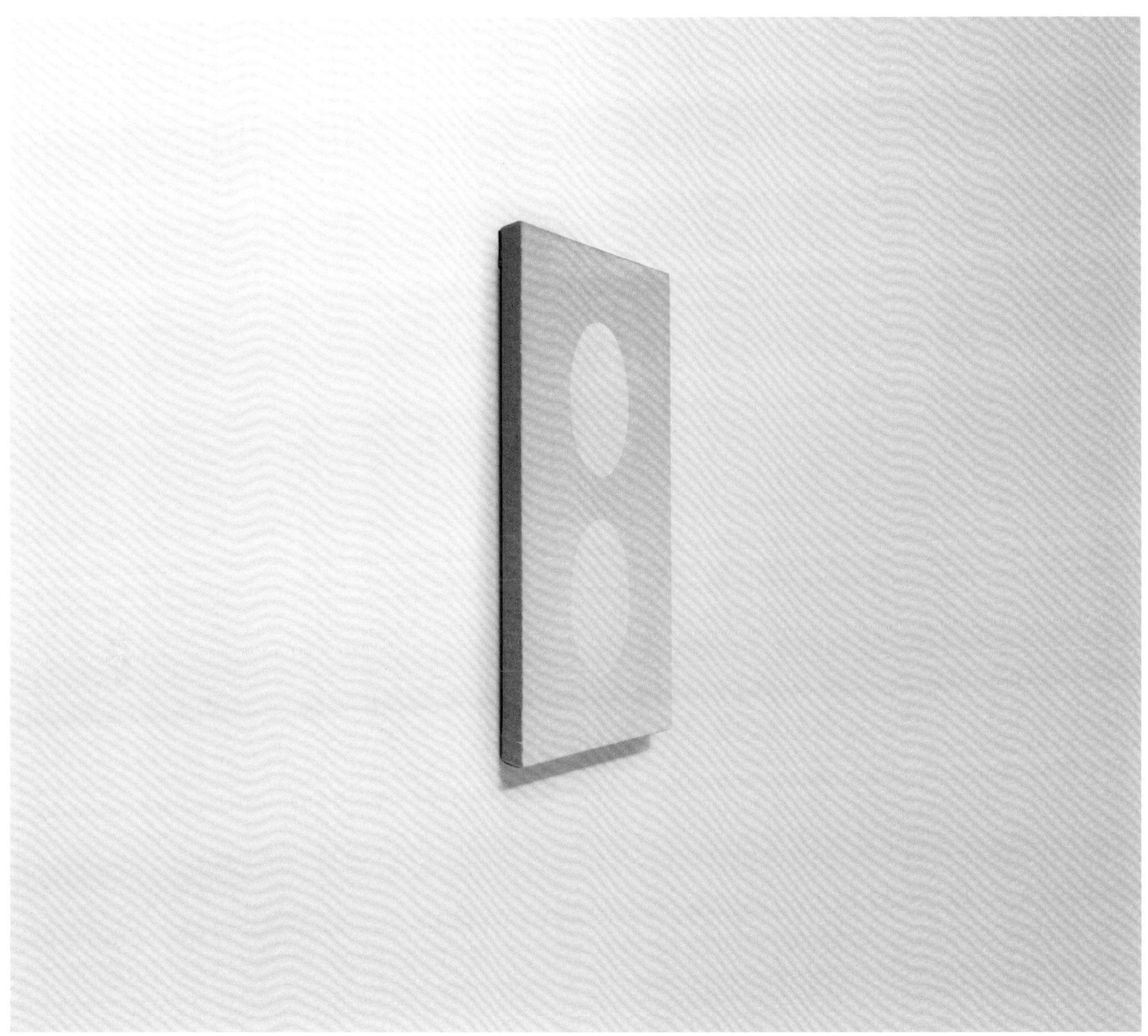

Bevel VII, 2015

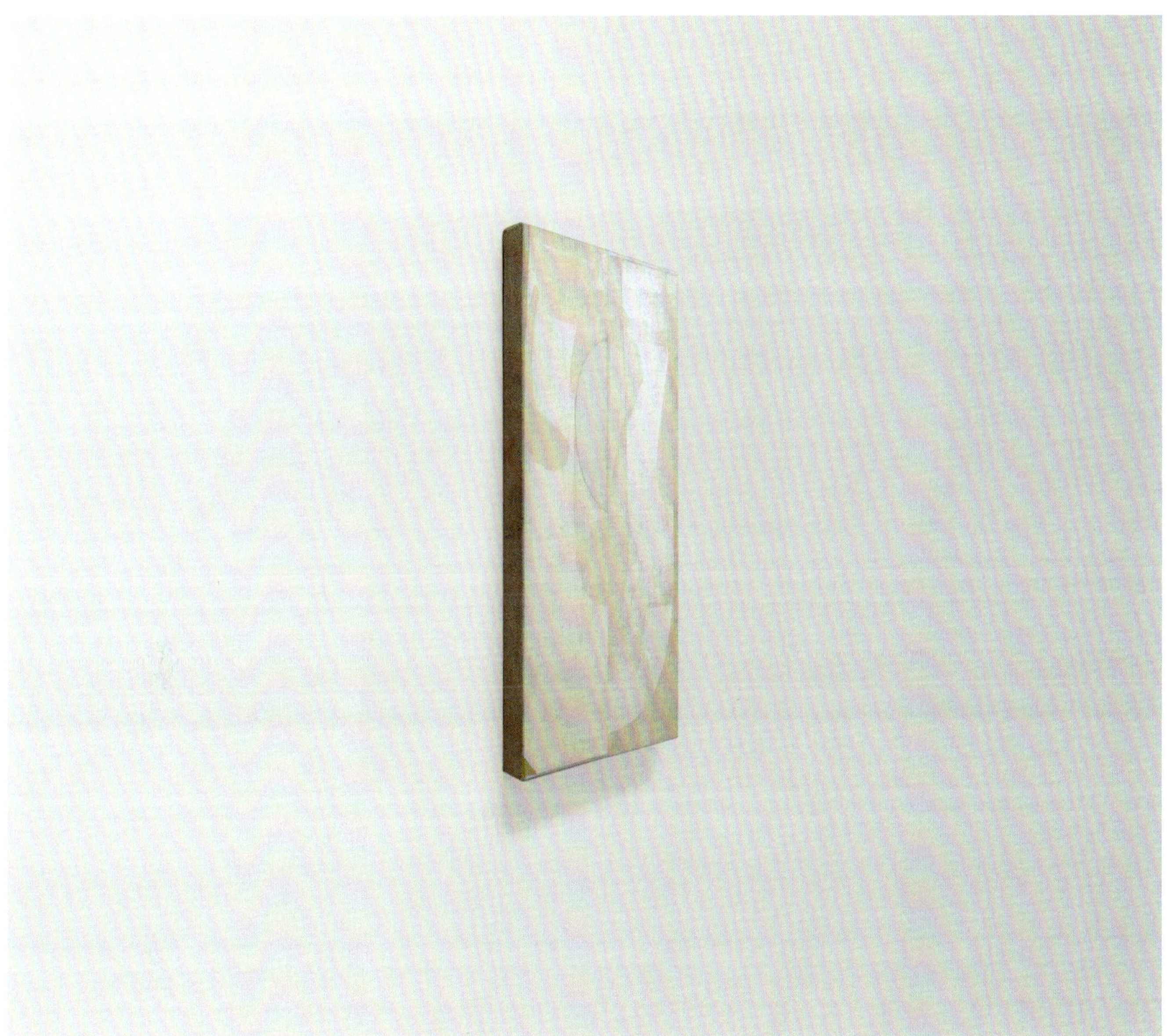

Near Infrared II, 2015

Near Infrared, 2015

Near Infrared III, 2015

Red Herring, 2015

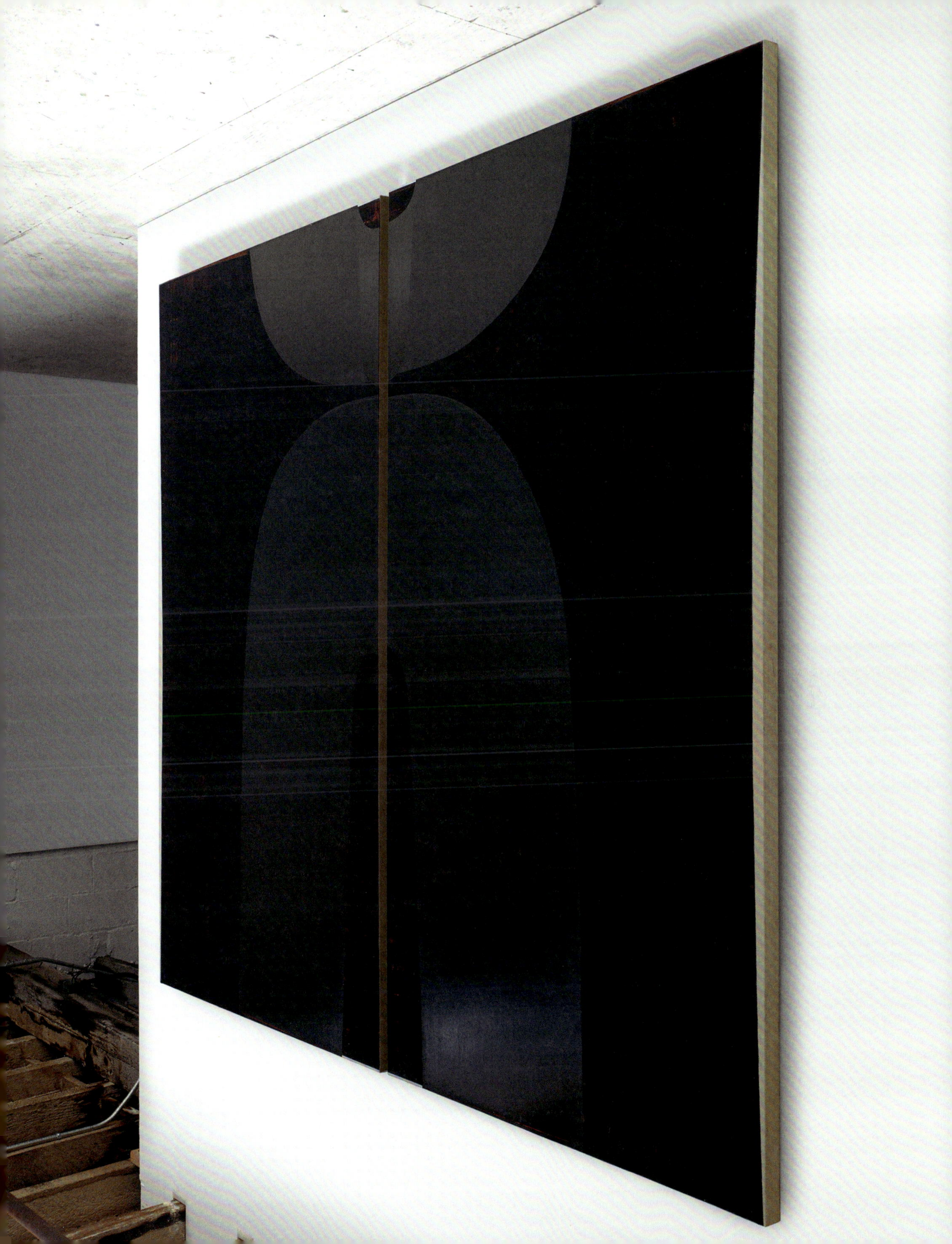

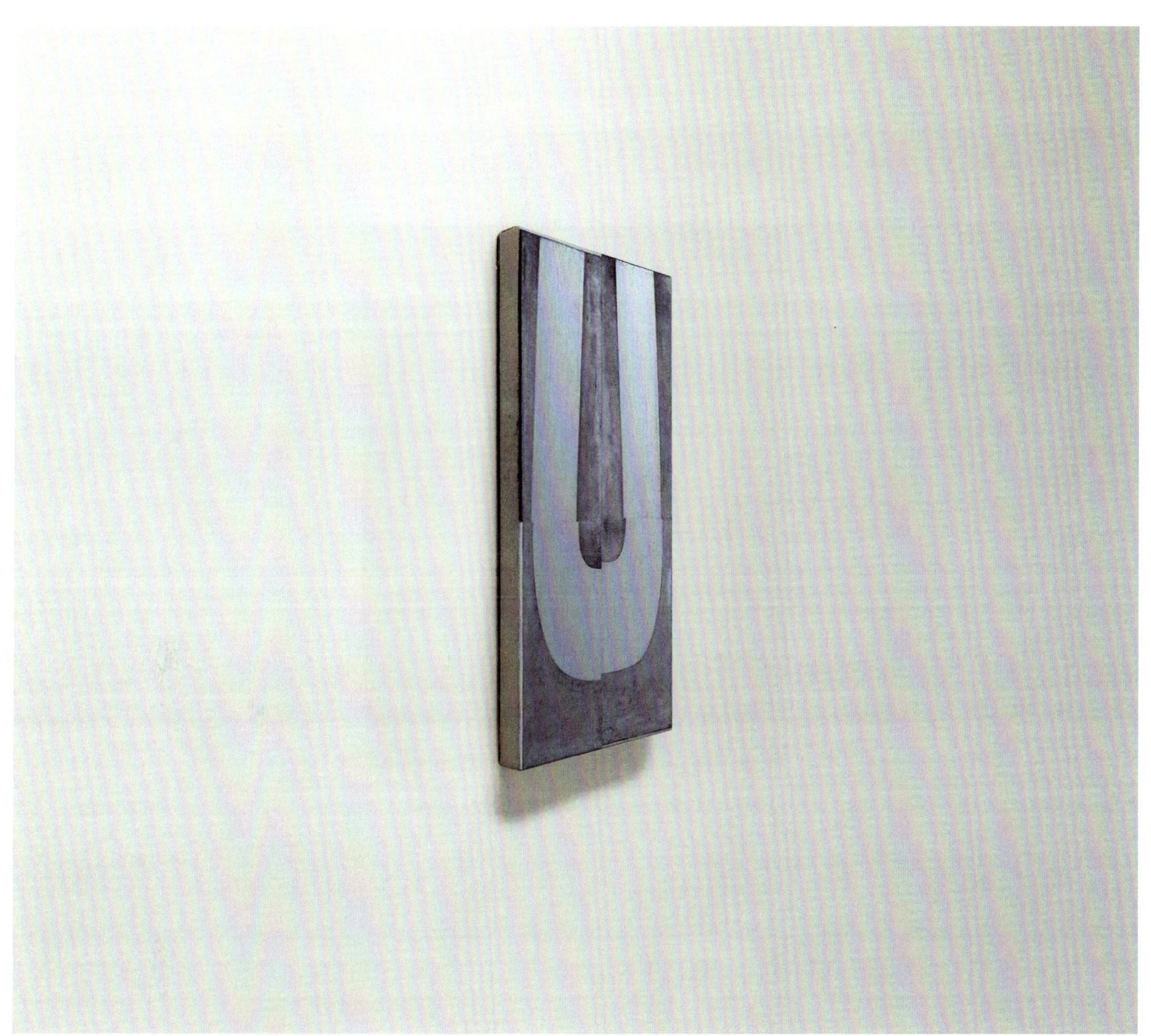

Near Ultraviolet II, 2015

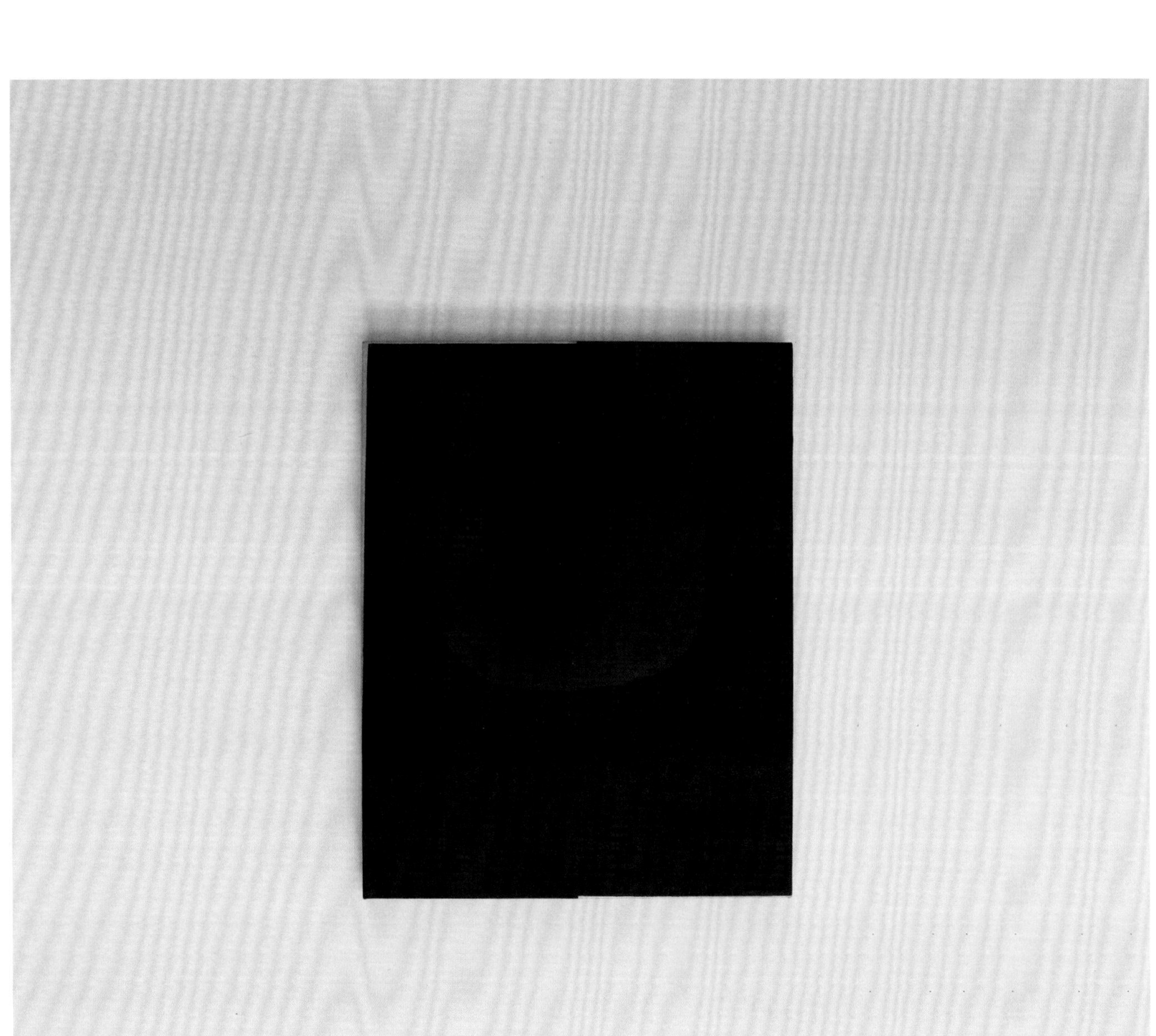

Near Ultraviolet, 2015

Straw Man, 2014

Doubleu (pale), 2014

Doubleu, 2013–2014

Loop, 2015

PROLOGUE

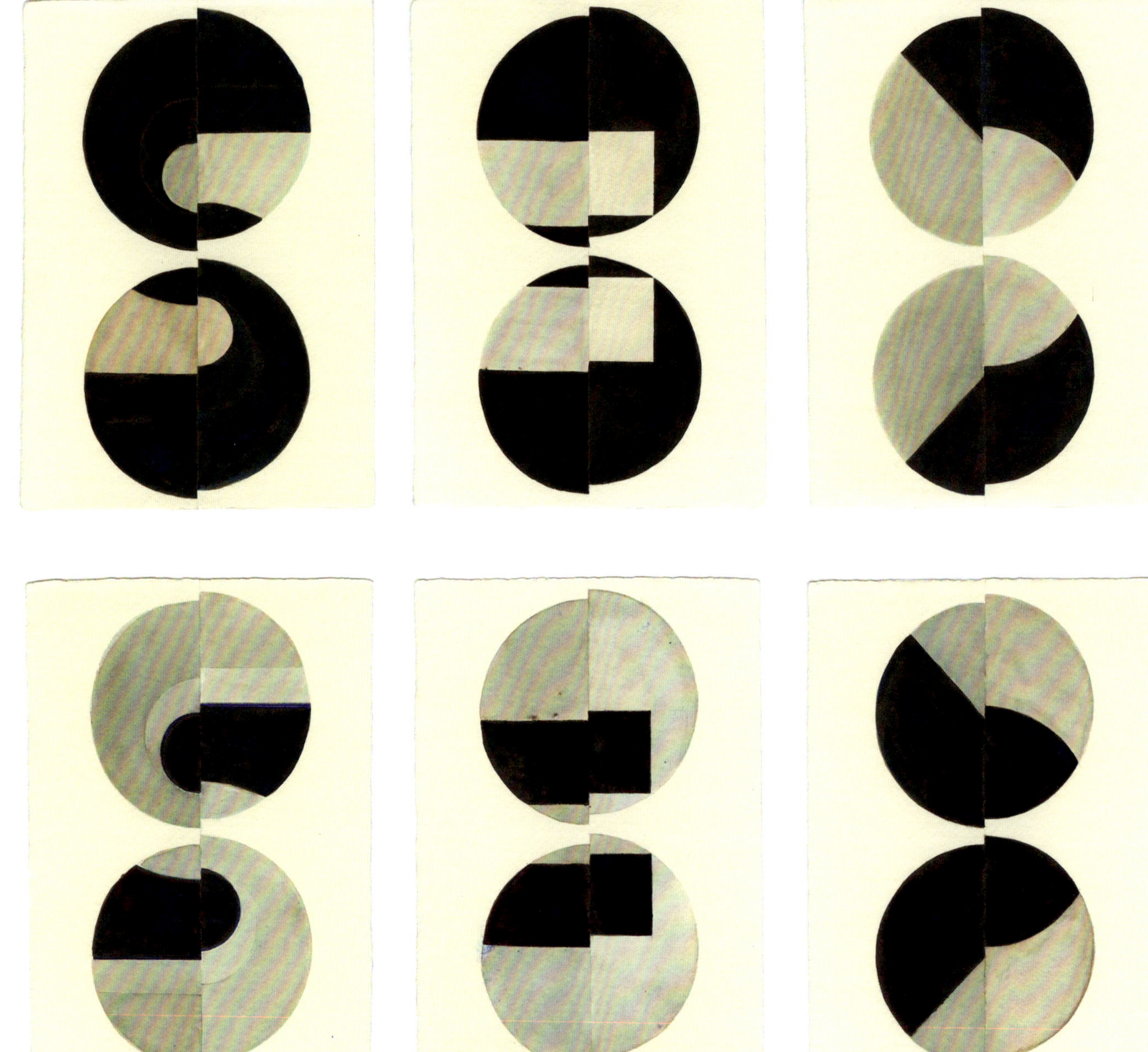

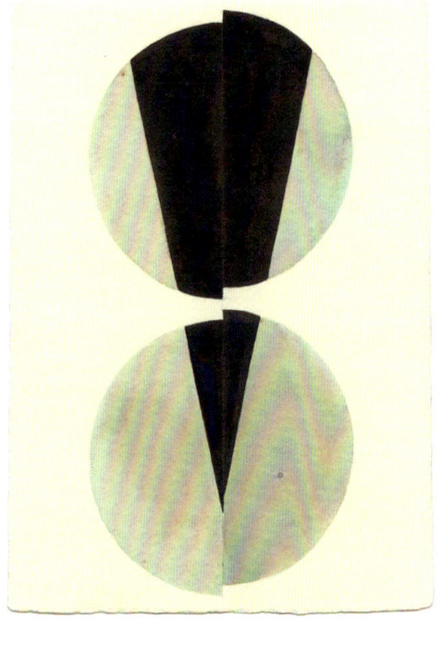
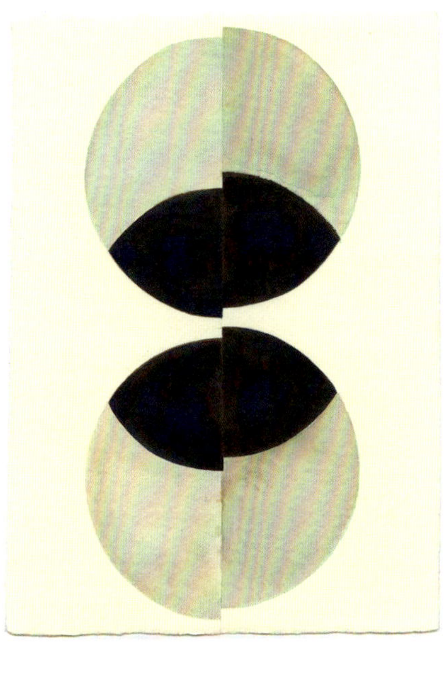
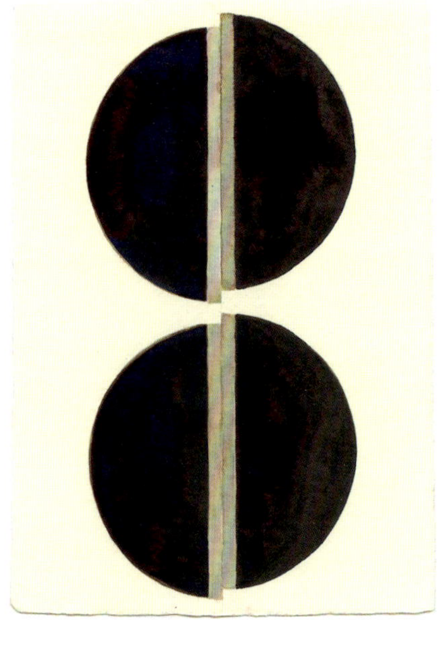
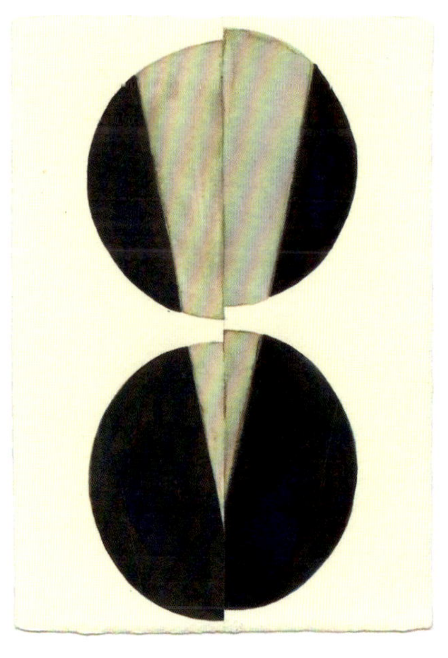
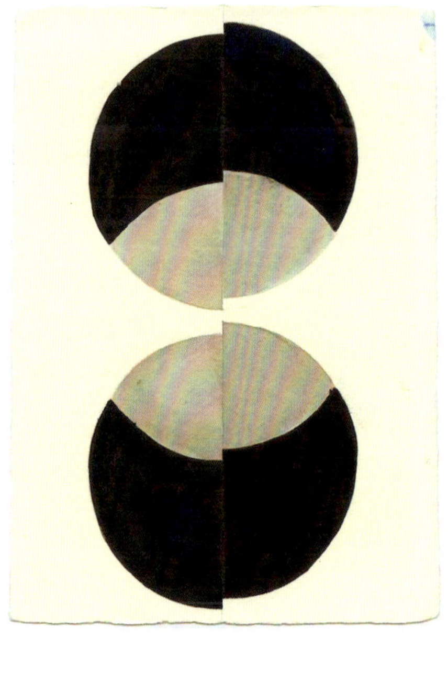
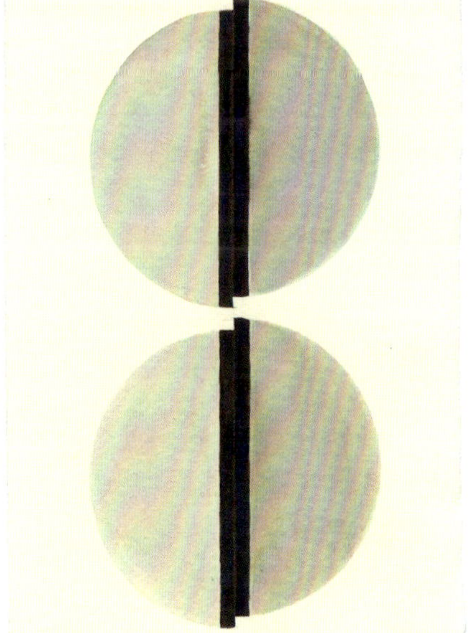

Top row: *Council, Untitled (16–25)*, 2016; Bottom row: *Council, Untitled (16–26)*, 2016
Watercolor and walnut ink on paper, 8 x 5¾ inches (21 x 15 cm)

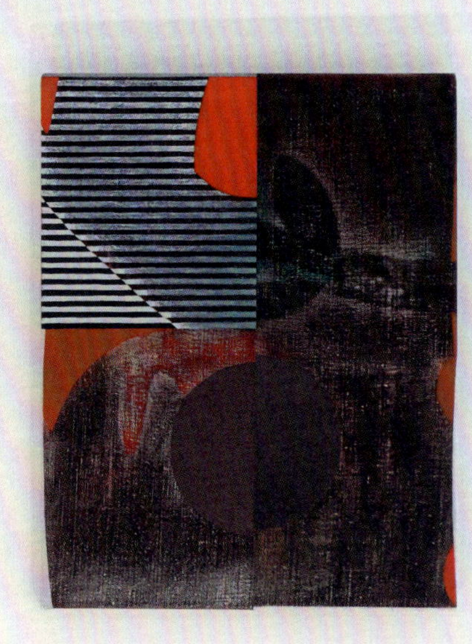

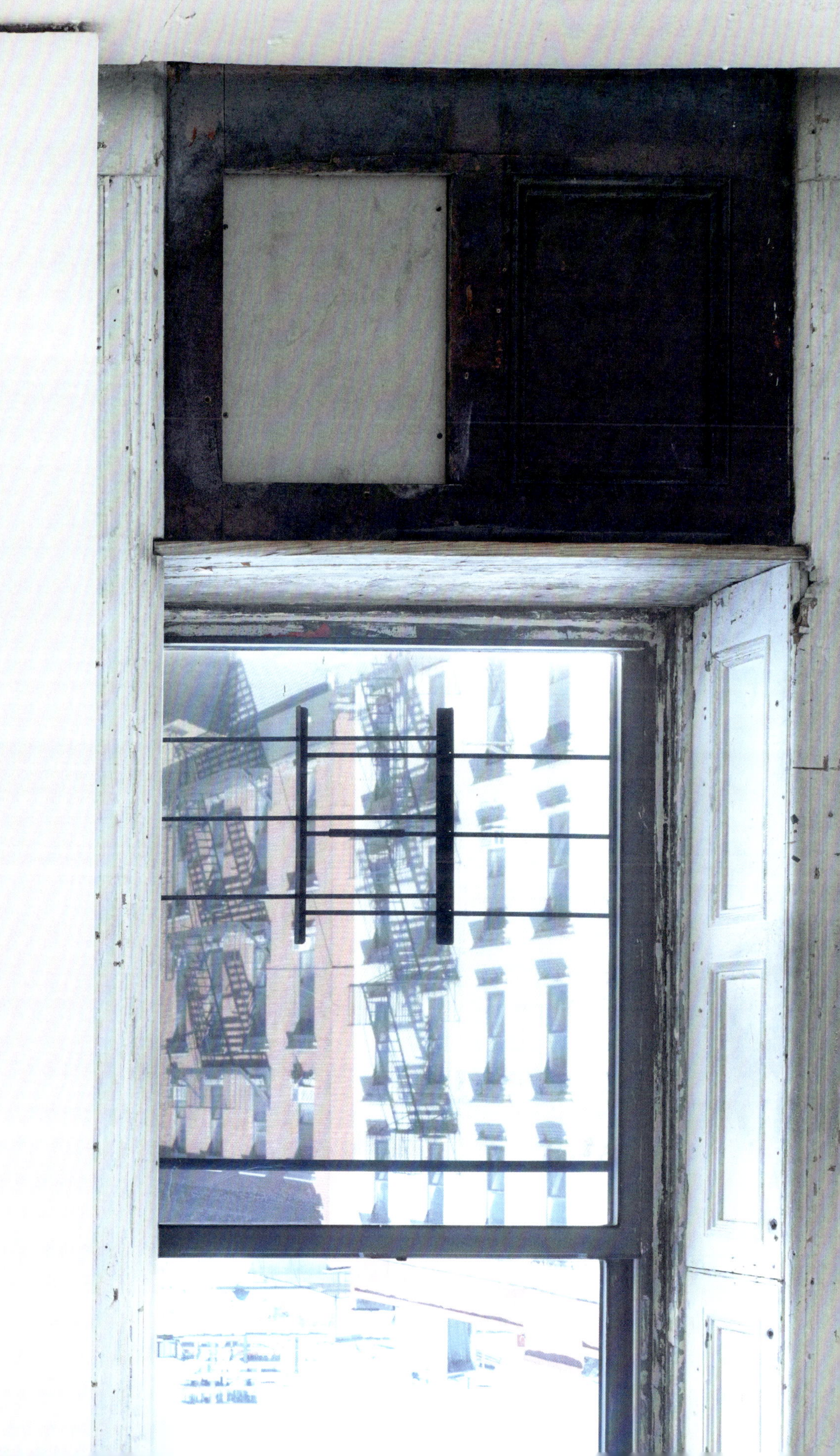

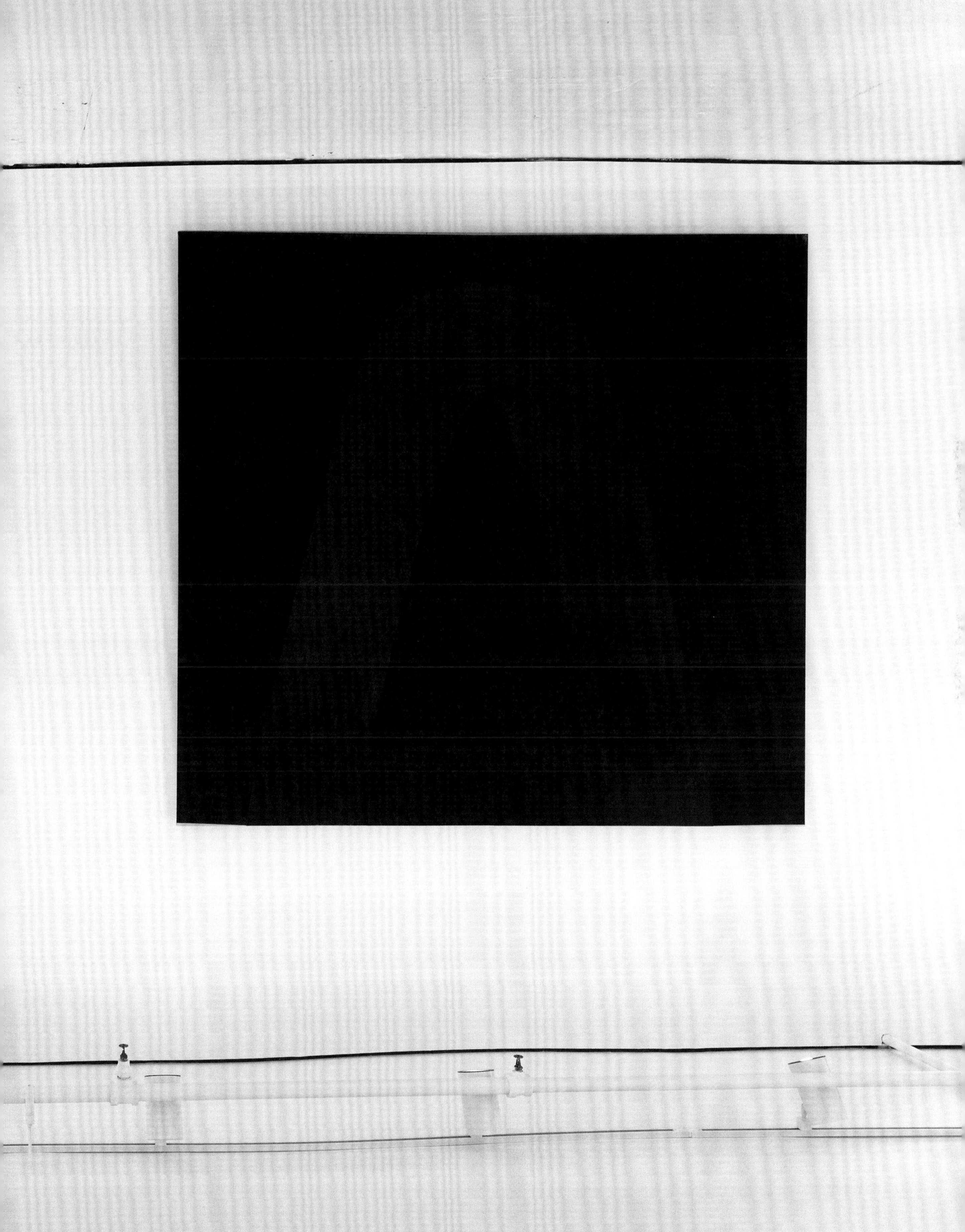

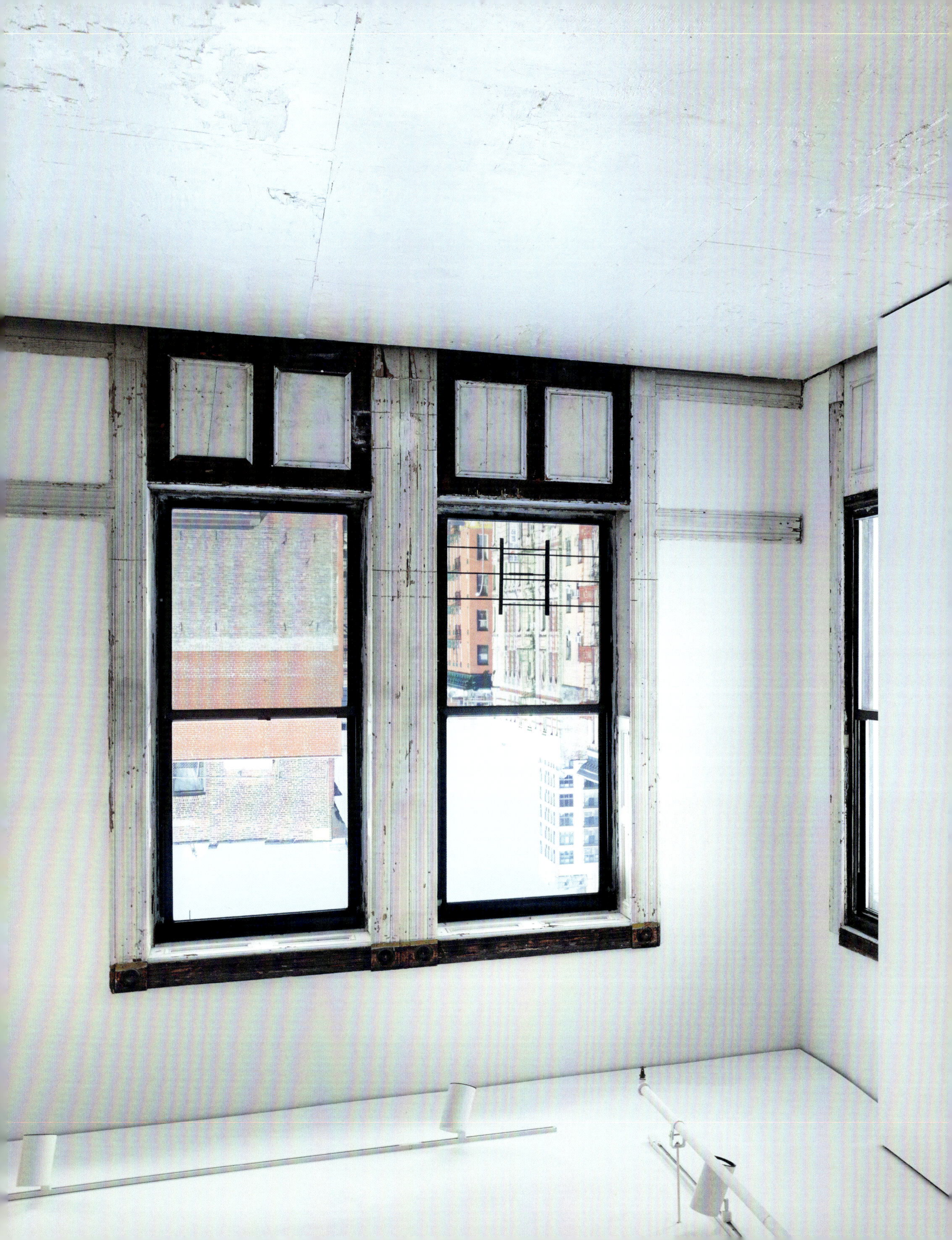

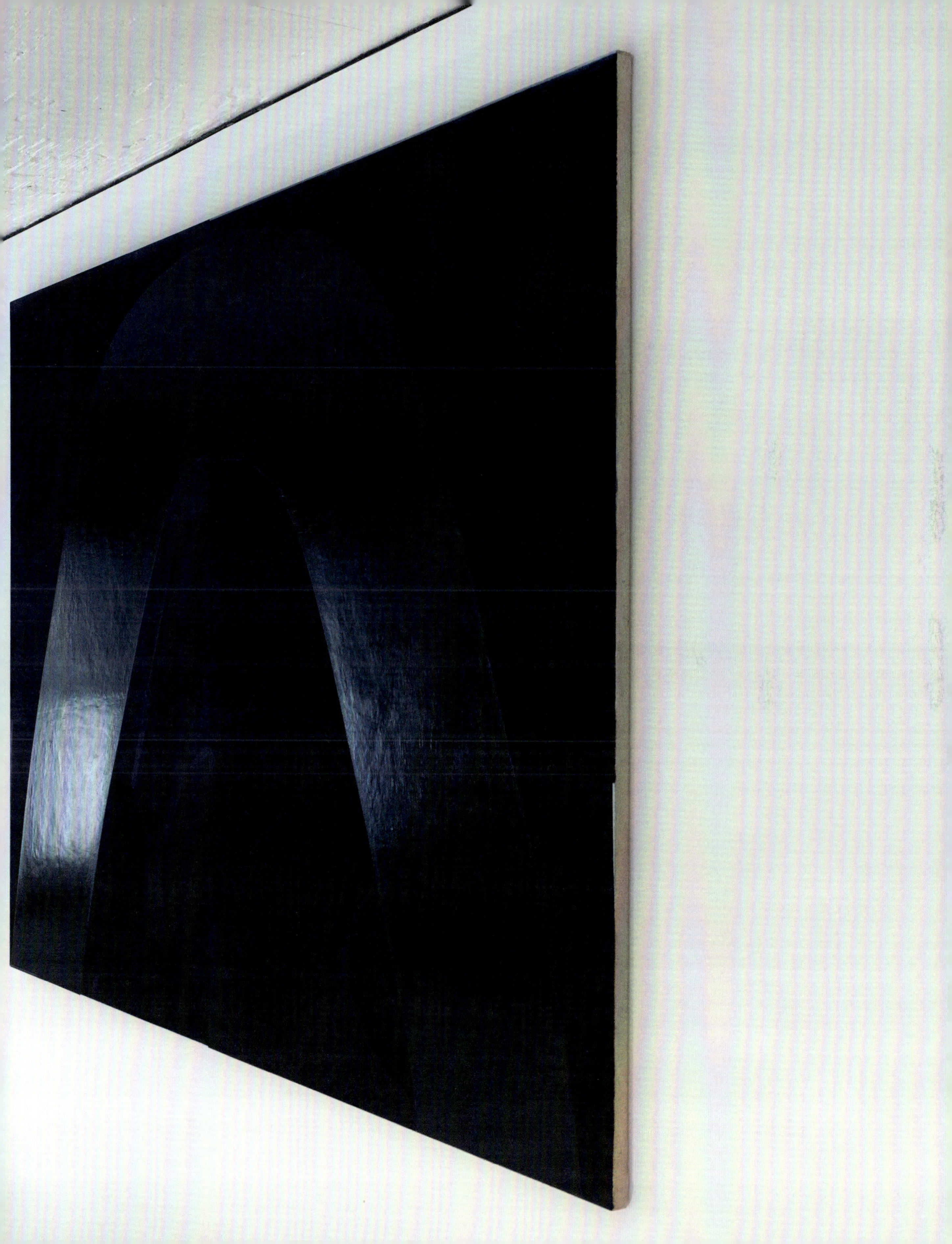

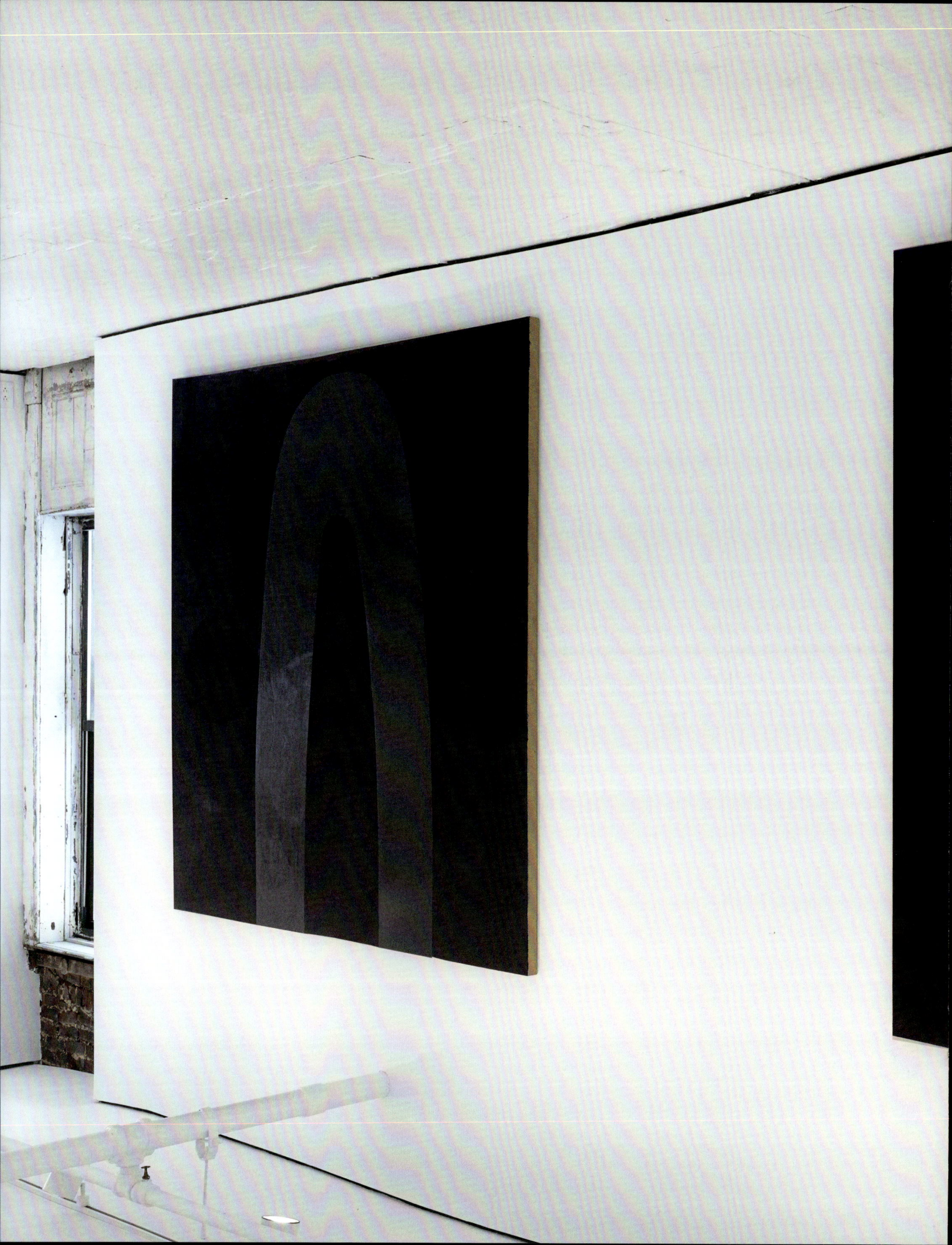

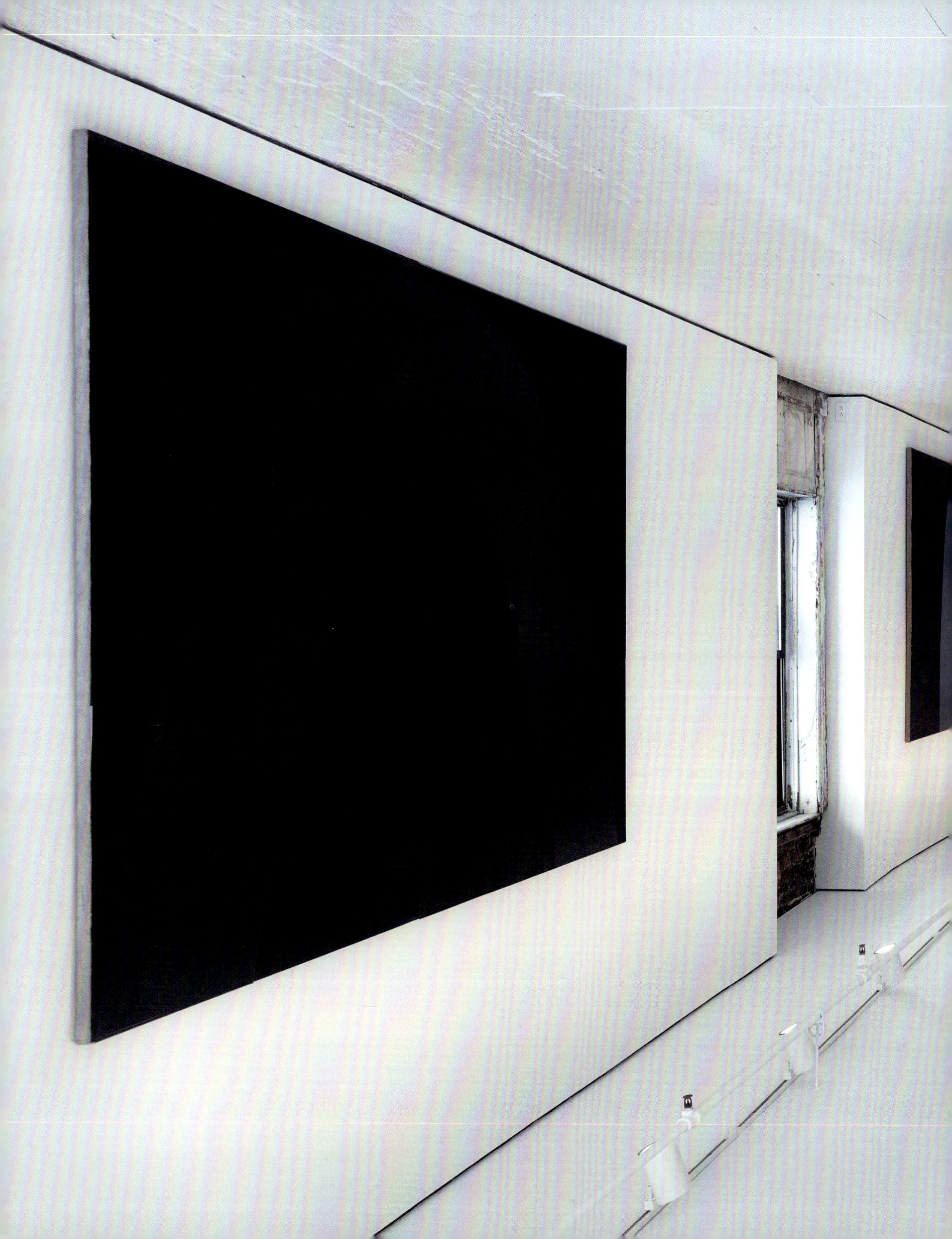

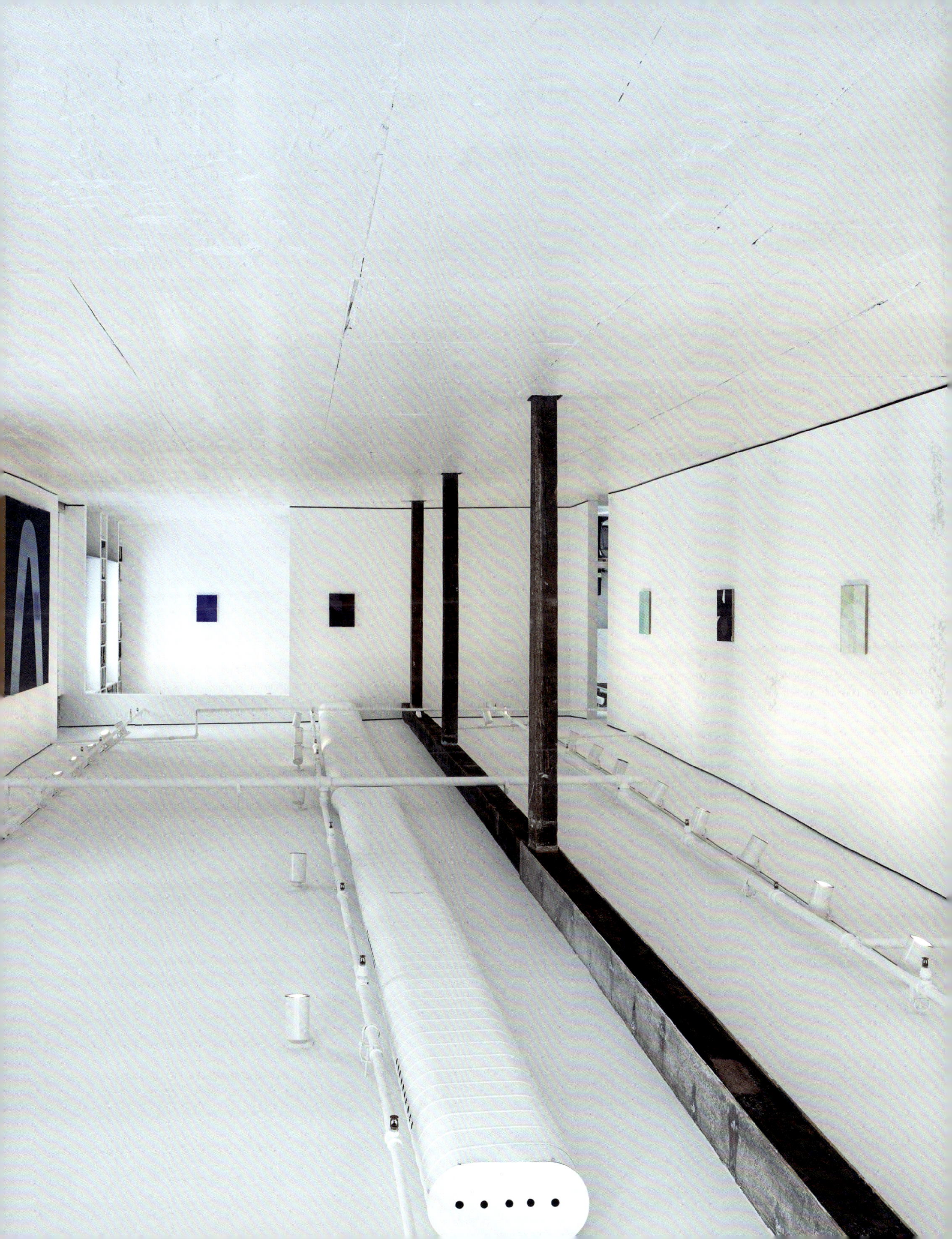

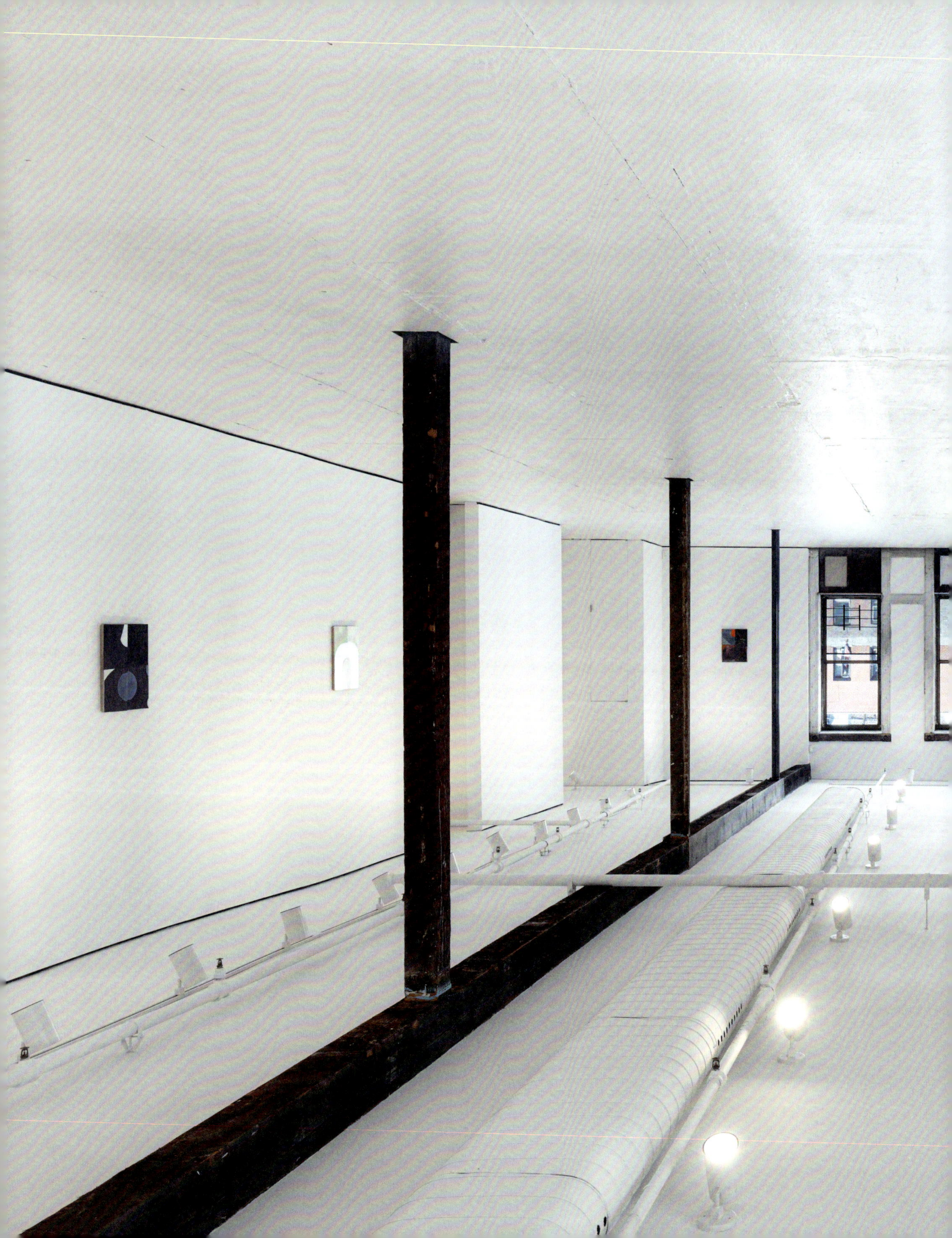

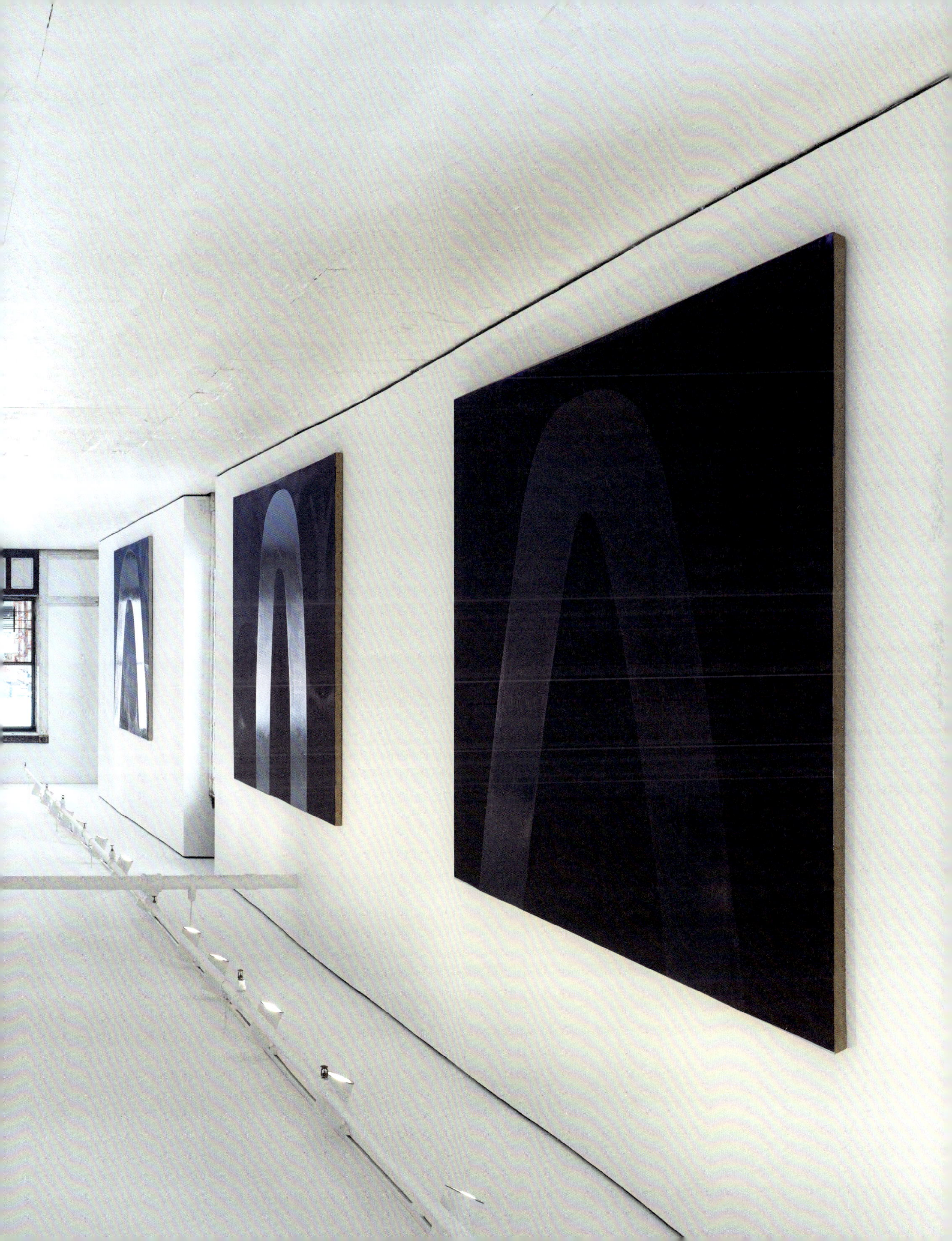

Resonance II, 2016

Resonance, 2016

Consonance II, 2016

Consonance, 2016

Assonance, 2016

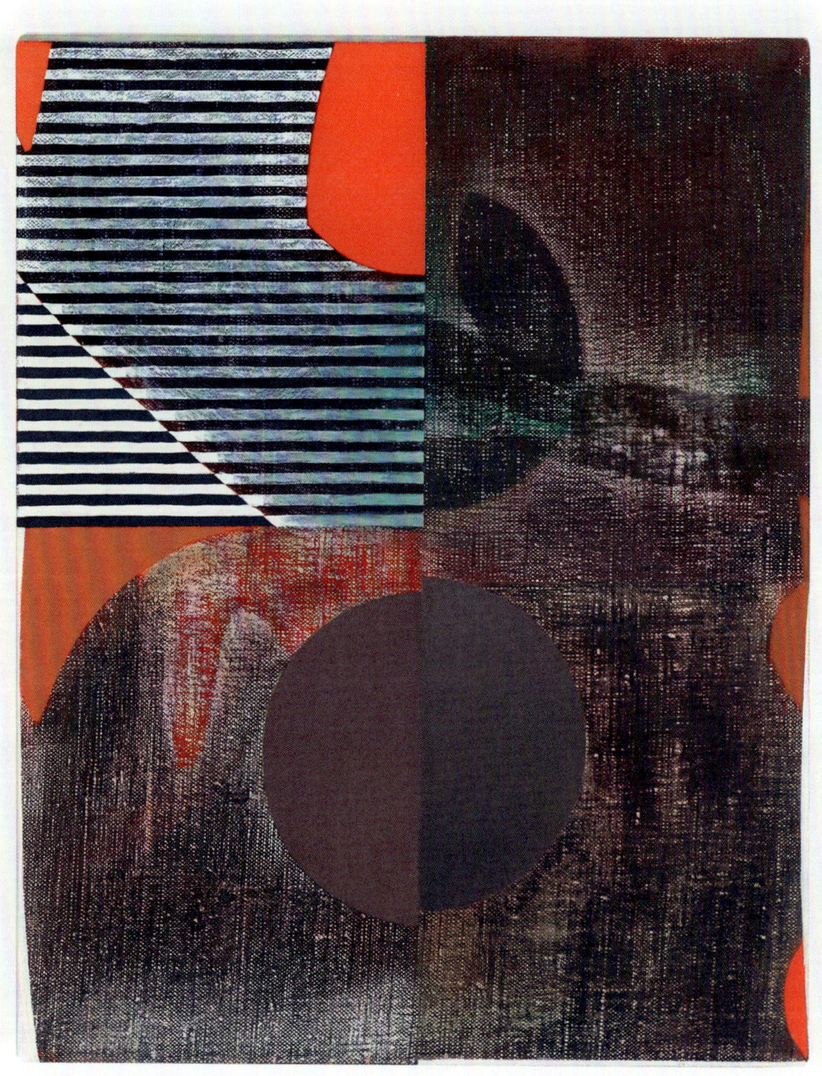

Dissonance, 2016

West, 2016

Gilles, 2014

Twice Six, 2016

(the third ear)

March 30 – May 15, 2016

NATHALIE KARG GALLERY, NEW YORK

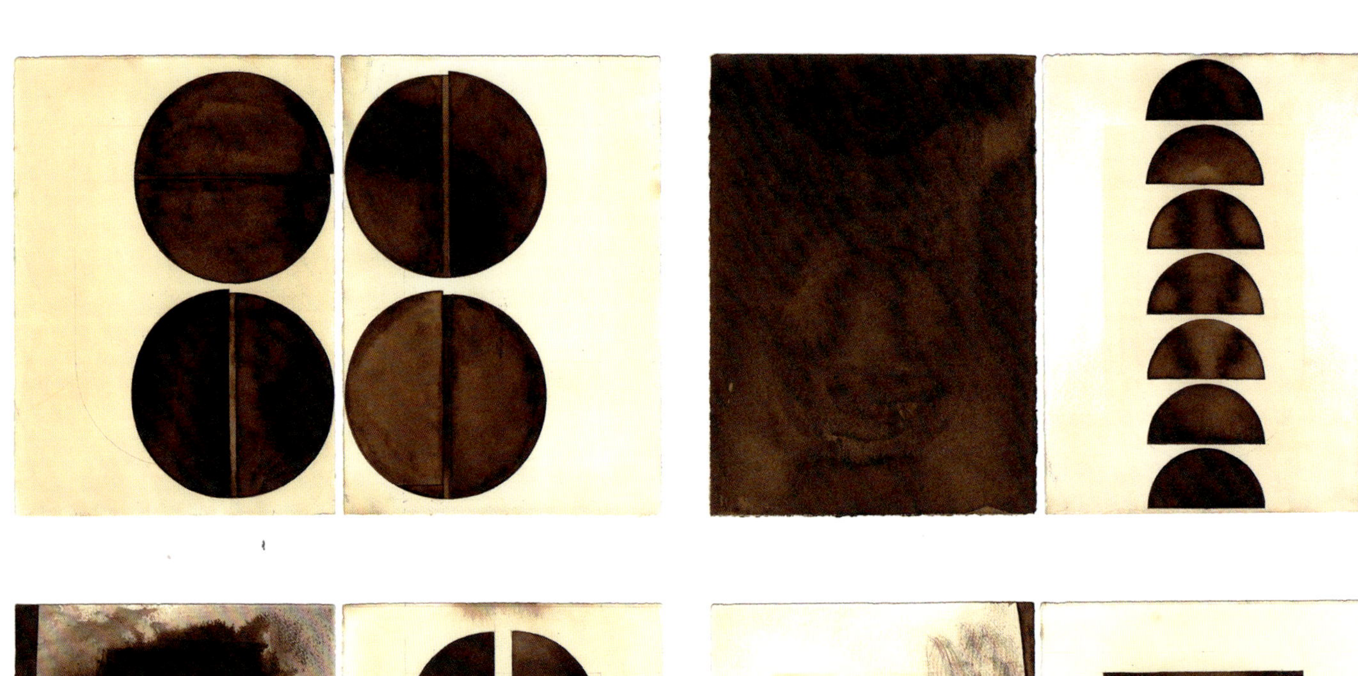

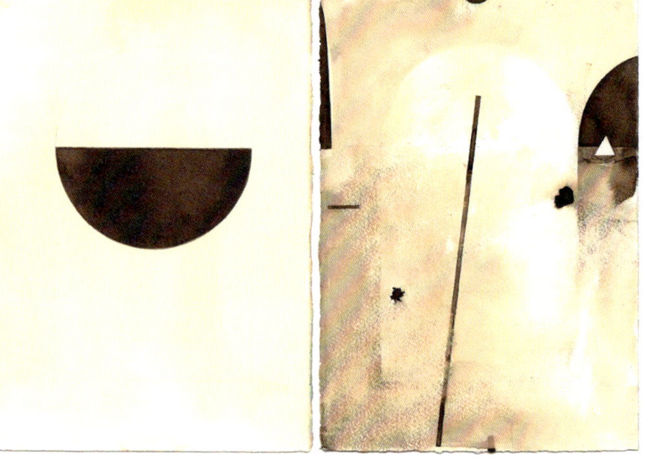
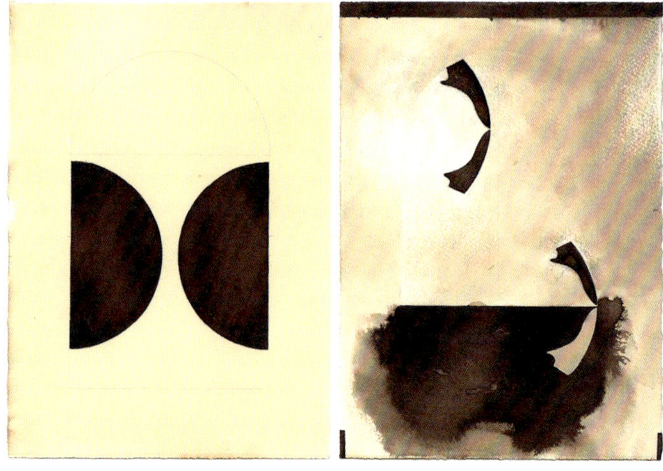
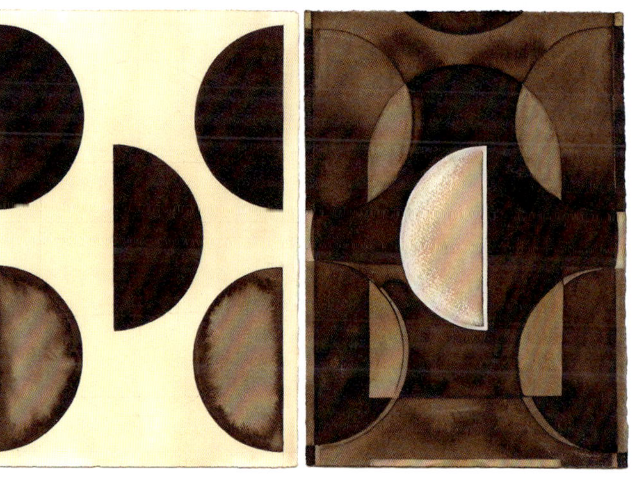
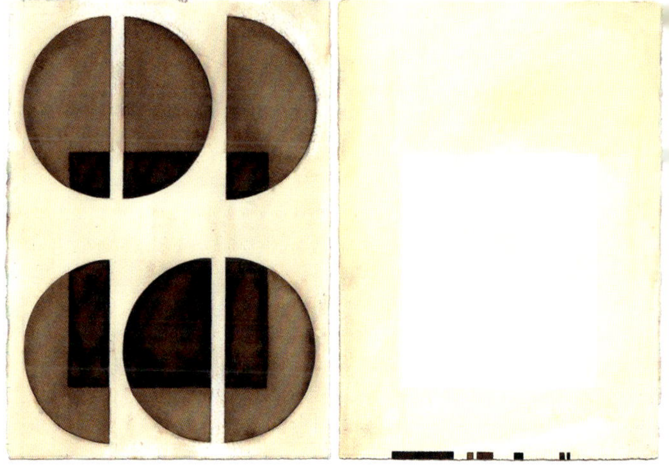

A Week and Its Seven Days: The Merging of Reason and Optical Intuition #1–8, 2012
Walnut ink on tea-stained paper, diptych, each sheet 11.8 x 8.5 inches, (30 x 21.5 cm)

On the other side of my desk hangs a small painting by Nathlie Provosty, from 2014. At just over a foot tall, it is the same height as the orchid. Like most of her paintings, in certain light, especially in artificial light, it appears to be just a dark rectangular monochrome. Its linen edges are stained umber, and there is a thin bevel slanting from the side to the face that glows the color of wine—a red ground that shines, almost imperceptibly, beneath the silken bronze paint covering the surface. Daylight raking through the windows initiates a narrative arc: in the morning three glossy half-circles appear, stacked vertically in the center. In the blaze of the afternoon these shapes are undeniable, making me wonder how I could ever mistake it for an imageless plane. By dusk, however, they've receded again, flashing into view only at certain angles. My experience of the painting changes not only with the day, but as I move throughout the room; grabbing a book or refilling my coffee shows me new aspects of it as a thing. It is the kind of painting that gets better—more meaningful, nuanced, and expansive—the more it becomes part of your everyday life.

Sitting here now, between that flower and that painting, I suspect I've set them up as a kind of frame—conceptual bookends—to teach myself something about paying attention—about the nature and the qualities of attention, as it unfolds in time.

middle, with slight disjuncture at the center. The warping spatial effect of this is amplified by the small adjustments Provosty maneuvers onto every canvas's edge: subtly adding a light grey band, or tiny blue curve to a corner, which slices the overall shape in our perception—bending either backward or forward like an illusion, or a faint visual buzzing.

* * *

The family of small paintings in this exhibition are all 19 by 15 inches. While each is individual, they are all paired: *Dissonance* and *Assonance*; *Resonance* and *Resonance II*; *Consonance* and *Consonance II*. Because they share a basic composition, looking at their differences allows you to understand their deeper structure, a distant ur-image, the way a diamond's faceted surface relates to its molecular architecture. The titles hint at Provosty's compositional strategy: assonance, dissonance and consonance are literary devices for constructing rhythm in poetry or prose through sound—assonance by repetitive vowel sounds, consonance with harmonic consonants, and dissonance is the inverse of these two, purposely suppressing the effects of internal and external repetition.

Dissonance was the first of the group, and its elements appear more disparate than any of the others. There is a center dividing line and two joined semi-circles meeting at the top center. The right side is a dark orangey taupe and the left is cooler and greener. This broken circle appears smoothed on top of the linen, which has been sanded and scrubbed down around it to leave an undulating plane of colors embedded in the thick weave. The lower right quadrant is striped in alternating dark and light, and appears to be exact, but upon approach the edges gently waver. An electric red-orange form sits on the lower edge of the stripes. The overall composition is almost an "R" shape, from which the rest of the paintings were elaborated. Though, sometimes, as in *Consonance*, the central upper circle melts into the painting, articulating the interior curve of a horseshoe, showing the jagged relationship between the four quadrants more clearly.

* * *

Up close, Provosty's surfaces radiate a particularly intense quality of care—not obsessive or oppressive, but just—a sense that everything has been properly considered and exactly attended to. This elicits meaning from the tiniest details: every distinction of sheen has been purposefully calibrated; each adjustment of the edge has a function in its larger mysterious scheme. They create faith that all is as it should be within their world, even as they remain elusive.

* * *

An orchid sits on a bookcase to the left of my writing desk—its petals the size of thumbprints, its leaves big as slightly cupped hands. The flowers are bright magenta, dark and velvety in the center, with rubbery leaves of a somewhat milky green. I have to stay aware of it for it to stay alive: making sure it has enough water and just the right amount of sun. It also teaches how to care by degrees; it doesn't want too much water, sun or attention—that will kill it just as fast. It gets moved from table to sill, watered weekly, and misted periodically. In exchange for all this care is its palpable presence. Peter Schjeldahl perfectly captures the peculiar quality of its existence when he says, "having an orchid is like having a very, very, very quiet pet."

Intuition, a cycle of eight diptychs in walnut ink, which derive their armature from the Limbourg brothers' *Très Riches Heures du Duc de Berry* (1412–1416). As the presence of this famous allegory of time suggests, much of Provosty's work deals with temporality—symbolically and phenomenally—searching for ways to enact both the collapse and passage of time within the experience of the visual field.

It's interesting to re-read four years later, seeing what an important work *A Week and Its Seven Days* turned out to be in the evolution of Provosty's art. These eight diptychs represent the first time she worked in a conscious series, now a key element of her paintings, which she sometimes calls "sets" or "families." The diptych form also remains a constant structural component—central underlying division—even if now it is often a submerged separation. Here, each set represents her attempt to reconcile the differences between the "intuitive or tactile" and "rational or measured" aspects of her visual vocabulary. The sumptuous dark brown walnut ink, pooling organically within the pristine geometric shape, illustrates one level of this marriage.

* * *

I've always liked Jacques-Emile Blanche's painting of Marcel Proust that hangs in the Musée d'Orsay—a portrait of the artist as a young flower. It is also a black painting; Marcel's suit and the background are both relatively unarticulated darknesses, though easily separated by tone. The pale oval of twenty-one-year-old Marcel's face hovers in the center. His face and shirt are almost the same color as the ghostly orchid pinned to the left side of his jacket. Every aspect of this dandy is orchidaceous: precious and sensitive, bringing to mind J. K. Huysman's description of orchids as "so delicate and charming, at once cold and palpitating, exotic flowers exiled in the heated glass palaces of Paris, princesses of the vegetable kingdom living in solitude."

It is a painting that delights in muted asymmetries, which is, of course, the formal relationship between orchids and human faces: a tour-de-force of almost unconsciously skewed bilateral equivalences. For instance, while the dark irises of Marcel's large eyes are parallel, the surrounding heavy lid is faintly lower on his left side, mirrored below by the small slight-off wings of his shirt collar. While human and orchid faces both appear to be arranged on a central plane, they are in fact clustered compound curves, making the business of locating all the slight imbalances a slow process of unfolding.

Nathlie Provosty's paintings are constructed of exactly these kinds of illusive doublings, partial echoes and combined shadow-shapes, which lead you around the painting. Take *West* for example, its central sweeping "U" shape is a stable division of the rectangle. But beneath its satiny uppermost layer glimmers a subdivision in color and sheen: the canvas appears to have been once divided down the middle—the memory of a diptych past. Carved out of the darkness on the lower left and right side, seemingly mirrored over a central axis, is a strange three-pronged shape, like a bird's foot. They are not inversions of each other, but the product of some cryptic transposition. There is a similar sequence of chiming arcs climbing up the left and right side of the "U." The overall effect is like a Victorian translation of an epic poem, alternating rhyming couplets of slightly slanted rhythms, that add up, almost by surprise, to something startlingly grand.

While *Gilles*, *West*, and *Twice Six* all share the central "U," each uses it to contort space in a different way: *Gilles* is the narrowest, pulled tight into the center, almost like a vase. Closer looking reveals that *West*'s "U" slopes slightly right, creating an unmistakably physical sense of imbalance; and *Twice Six*'s is the widest and the least symmetrical, thickening near its curved

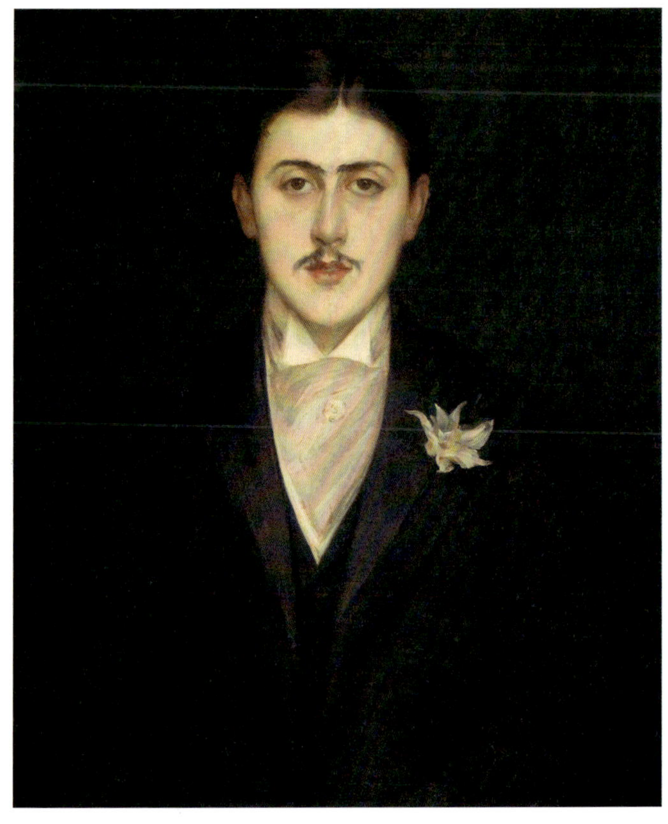

Jacques-Emile Blanche, *Portrait de Marcel Proust*, oil on linen, 1892
Courtesy of the Musée d'Orsay

LESSONS IN DARKNESS

BY JARRETT EARNEST

She had in her hand a bunch of cattleyas, and Swann could see, beneath the film of lace that covered her head, more of the same flowers fastened to a swansdown plume. She was wearing, under her cloak, a flowing gown of black velvet, caught up on one side so as to reveal a large triangular patch of her white silk skirt, with an 'insertion,' also of white silk, in the cleft of her low-necked bodice, in which were fastened a few more cattleyas. — Marcel Proust, *Swann's Way*

At first glance, Nathlie Provosty's paintings appear inescapably black, like cartoon holes or thick velvet drapes. Once your eyes acclimatize to their presence, you perceive sumptuous indigos, violets, and umbers. Her paintings make me dream of the richer vocabulary for darkness our language once had. According to the great historian of color Michel Pastoreau, Old and Middle English distinguished between *swart* (dull black) and *blaek* (luminous black)—a subtle, critical distinction that is Provosty's chief compositional device. Dull and luminous darknesses embody specific meanings in what, for Provosty, amounts to a philosophical meditation.

Three large paintings, *Gilles*, *West*, and *Twice Six*, measure seven feet high by nearly eight feet wide. They feel both bodily and architectural, scaled like majestic double-doors interceding between the figure and the room. Each has the central image of a wide "U" shape, defined only by a difference in sheen: glossy on matte, like the track of a giant snail. From some angles it shines with platinum light, the way wet asphalt reflects the sky after a storm. Though closely related, the color-feeling of each painting differs. *West* is plummy, a swelling, cold purple. *Gilles* is bluer: luminous indigo rustling through dim navy. And *Twice Six* is more like slate, like the back of a mirror, afire with orange undertones verging on iridescence.

* * *

At the end of 2012 Nathlie Provosty had an exhibition called *Book of Hours* at *1:1*, the alternative space I ran with three friends on Essex Street. Provosty's was the only straight painting show in our year-long experiment, which included everything from installations of Peter Lamborn Wilson's altars, to performances like *Spit Banquet*, with bodily fluids galore. In that show's press release, I wrote:

Nathlie Provosty's recent work is the product of deep meditation on underlying forms throughout history. Recalling Aby Warburg's *Mnemosyne Atlas*, she gathers thousands of images, arranging them into groups and subgroups, analyzing their inherent geometric structure and its relationship to the emotional content of the image. From that research, she derives basic forms which become the skeletons of her abstract paintings—sensitive and complex. Included in the exhibition is the major work *A Week and Its Seven Days: The Merging of Reason and Optical*

pp. 2–3: *Council, Untitled (15-52)–(15-57)*, 2015

p. 6: Exhibition view with *Twice Six*, Nathalie Karg Gallery, New York

CONTENTS

9 LESSONS IN DARKNESS

17 *(the third ear)*

36 INSTALLATION VIEWS

57 PROLOGUE

100 LIST OF PLATES

103 BIOGRAPHY

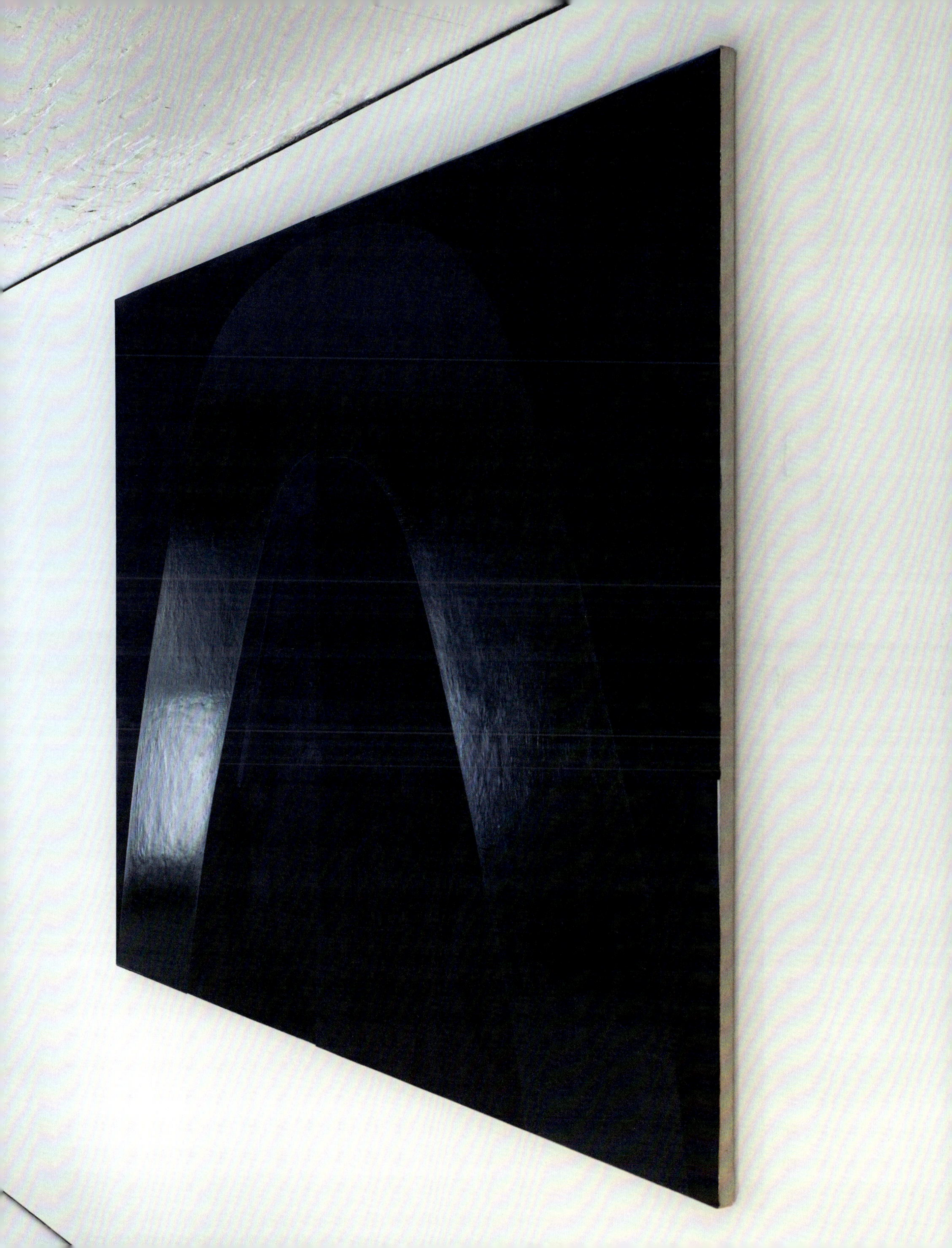

NATHLIE PROVOSTY

DISTANZ

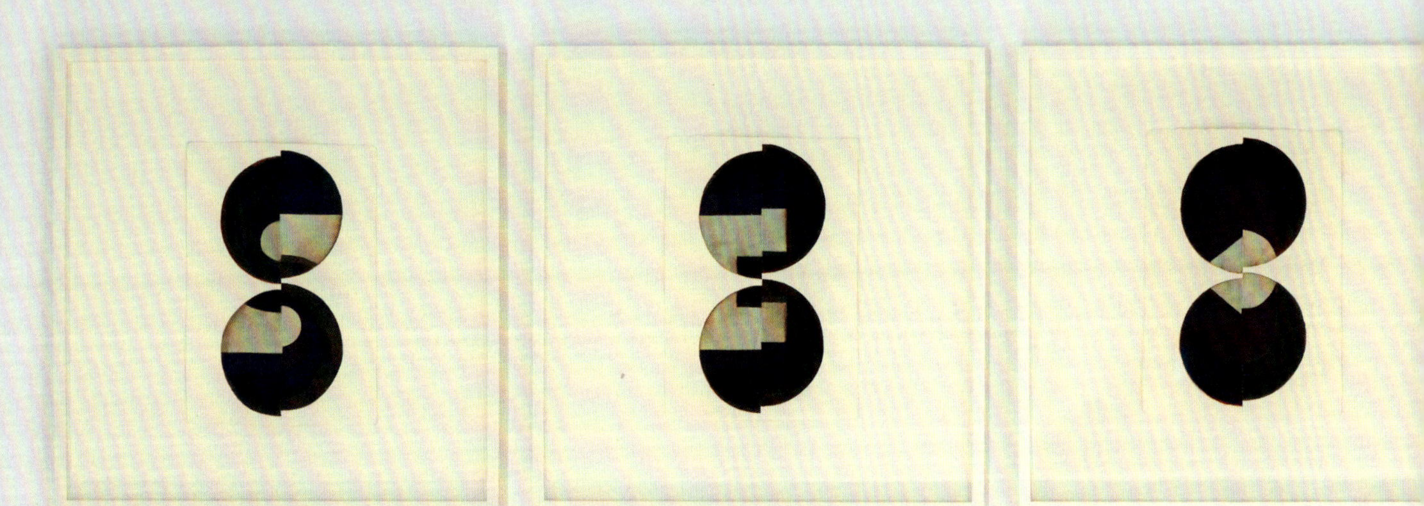

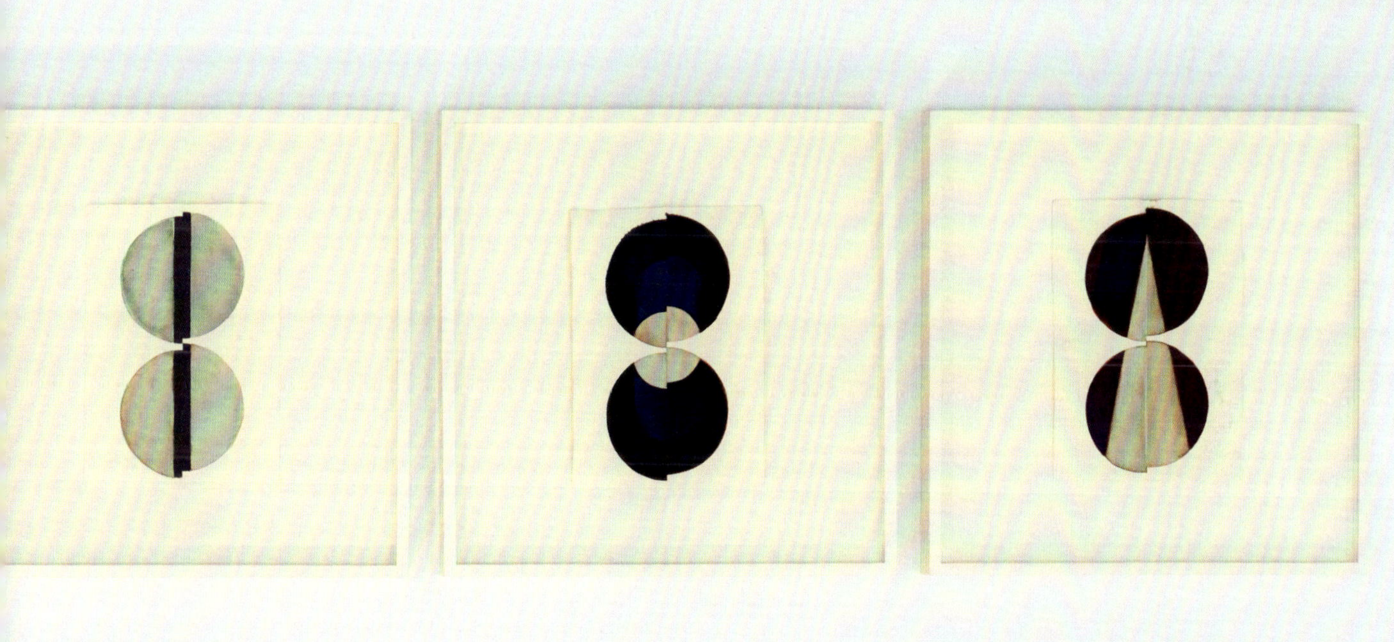

NATHLIE PROVOSTY